A New Dawn in the Millennium

Religious Mythologies - A Threat to World Peace and Personal Freedoms

by

William B. Fotheringham

Bloomington, IN   Milton Keynes, UK
authorHOUSE®

AuthorHouse™
1663 Liberty Drive, Suite 200
Bloomington, IN 47403
www.authorhouse.com
Phone: 1-800-839-8640

AuthorHouse™ UK Ltd.
500 Avebury Boulevard
Central Milton Keynes, MK9 2BE
www.authorhouse.co.uk
Phone: 08001974150

First published by AuthorHouse 5/2/2008

ISBN: 978-1-4184-7031-9 (e)
ISBN: 978-1-4184-5325-1 (sc)

Printed in the United States of America
Bloomington, Indiana

This book is printed on acid-free paper.

DEDICATION

To my wife, Laura, for not only tolerating all the male chores of our household that went undone while I pounded on the keyboard, but also for her willingness, as an agnostic, to be my favorite critic of this writing--our biggest obstacle to an organized household.

Each time I finished a chapter, she was available to challenge my arguments. As an avid reader, she found articles that she thought needed to be included in this book, and she offered criticism from a reader's standpoint. It was her viewpoint that gave title to this book.

WHY I WROTE THIS BOOK

The motivation for writing this book began one day when I was flipping TV channels and I heard a leader of the Christian Channel say to a young woman, "How do you think that young virgin felt when she realized that she had God in her womb?"

That concept made me wonder how an educated adult could believe such fantasy. As I talked with ministers and priests, I found that the humanizing of Spirit, Love, Life, Truth and Intelligence in the physical body of Jesus was a common conception. The author's reaction to this belief was like that of a famous tennis player, "You can't be serious?" This book is a challenge for Christians to broaden their concept of God and drop anthropomorphism and idolatry as a point of prayer.

TWENTY QUESTIONS ASKED OF CHRISTIANS

1. Do you believe that Christianity is God's choice of religion and non-Christians are infidels?

2. Do you believe that every word in the Bible is the word of God?

3. Do you believe that God created the world and the universe in six days?

4. Do you believe that the story of Adam and Eve is factual?

5. Do you believe that the Trinity describes God?

6. Do you believe that Jesus is God?

7. Do you believe Jesus died for your sins so that now you will go to Heaven?

8. Do you believe that you are saved by declaring Jesus as your savior?

9. Do you believe that God has a will for every living being?

10. Do you believe that all humans are sinners and there is a sin that could offend God?

11. Do you believe that God and Jesus will fight the war of Armageddon?

12. Do you believe in the existence of Heaven, Hell and Satan?

13. Do you believe that there is eternal life after death but not before birth?

14. Do you believe that there should be government support for religion, and the First Amendment violates the funding of religion?

15. Do you believe that there should prayers in public schools?

16. Do you believe that God created women inferior to men?

17. Do you believe that adultery is an unforgivable sin?

18. Do you believe that God opposes abortion?

19. Do you believe that God opposes same-sex marriage?

20. Do you believe that sodomy is an unforgivable sin?

It is the author's opinion that logical answers will be given to these questions in this writing.

Table of Contents

FOREWORD

The purpose of this writing is to select simple guidelines for the determination of whether a dogma or doctrine promulgated by the Christian ministry will succeed in the millennium.

Religious mythologies are beliefs without proof and beliefs without logic. The Christians have God Jesus, God the Father, the Holy Spirit and God Jehovah as their God, and they believe in the deific powers of the Virgin Mary, but other than statements written in the Bible, there is not a shred of proof that any of these gods exist. Yet, many believers are willing to die to defend their beliefs. Many followers of the Muslim God have been taught that there must be an ineluctable Holy War against the great Satan, the United States. In this writing, Christians are challenged to consider the impact that mythological concepts have on the logic and purity of their Christian theology or on any other theology.

This writing is not to be construed as a religious machination of Christian doctrine. It is an exegesis of the ideological affect of biblical controversy surrounding the teaching of creationism versus evolution to the 21st century children. Children, as thinkers, are becoming increasingly technologically oriented and are demanding evidence based on logic and truth before there is conviction in doctrine and dogma. This presents a challenge to the common acceptance by the Christians of a humanized Deity, and through which the Muslim jihad is becoming a threat to world peace.

The jeremiad of religious doctrine lies not with the beauty of the prose or with the authoritative depiction, but rather with the basic concepts of pure logic and proof of authenticity. Obfuscation created by rituals, exhortation of sinners, the horror of Hell, the symbolism of Satan and the use of a dead language, all enforce blind conformity to piousness.

The whole theology of Christianity is based on Jesus and his accomplishments. Present-day Christian leaders seem to promulgate a learned helplessness on all born-again Christians by teaching them that, at the time of death, salvation in Heaven may be achieved vicariously if Jesus was accepted by each Christian as a personal savior. In the meantime, they are helpless Christians waiting for death and Jesus' decision to ascend them to Heaven.

As we enter the 21st century, religious doctrines are going to be challenged by the scientific community as to their veracities. Presently, the sole authority for dogma is the Holy Bible. When more than the Bible will be needed to prove the efficacy of their beliefs, what will Christians do?

There is an old adage that a college education changes one's thinking from cocksure ignorance to cognitive uncertainty. The first major step in theology may be to change religious concepts to cognitive uncertainty and place religious beliefs to the tests of logic, coherency of ideas and common sense. This may determine whether or not religious beliefs can withstand the scrutiny of a rational analysis and the test of truth.

No one on earth has absolute proof of the existence or operation of Deity. All religious beliefs, ideas and doctrines are originated by mortals. Therefore, it would seem absolutely necessary before any one accepts religious concepts as factual, they should be compared to the qualities of truth. If an idea is illogical and cannot be proved, why should it be believed as factual? There has been 2000 years of Christianity without the healing works of Jesus. Instead of proving their doctrine by their works, the various religious organizations use the printed word of the Bible as primary proof of doctrine and the works of healing as secondary or irrelevant. To counter their obdurate views of Deity as sanctified through biblical quotations, this writing used biblical passages to present biblical authority for two opposing views. If the Bible is the only authority for religious truth, how does one determine what is true?

According to the Bible, Jesus gave his instruction to the uneducated peasants; so it would seem that the doctrine all the churches should be promulgating is a very simple one. However, simplicity may have been buried through the centuries by man-made pompousness, complexities of rituals, elaborate pageantry, and clerical additions, such as the Trinity, the magnification of evil in Satan, Hell, and the view of death as a stepping stone to Heaven or Hell depending on the capricious decision of Jesus.

There also seems to be a lack of logic in the basic religious belief that life originates in the protoplasm of temporal matter. Then by some strange phenomenon, man develops thought processes after death that suddenly provide him with omniscience, perfection, joy and life in eternal matter.

There is no attempt by this writing to delineate a specific religion as right or wrong. There is an attempt to bring rationality to religious beliefs and to explore religious concepts for logic and consistency of ideas. This is especially important for parishioners who are mentally captive to illogical and indefensible doctrines.

There is a movement by the Christian Right in the United States to have their religious concept of "Creationism" rather than "Evolution" taught in all of the schools of this nation as the true act of God. This writing will apply a test of logic and common sense to the Creationism movement.

Clergymen encourage their parishioners to donate money for the growth and influence of their particular church. It is through these donations that churches are able to survive in a country where freedom of religion is protected by law. The movement against the separation of church and state by the Christian Right is substantiated by articles from the Seattle Times, the New York Times and various books on the subject including the Americans United for the Separation of Church and State.

Unfortunately, there is no protection by law for those parishioners who are being misled into believing that payment to their church will ensure God's pleasure and their place in Heaven. Or by not declaring one allegiance to Jesus, one may be ostracized from God's inner circle, may incur God's anger, may not be admitted to Heaven, or may incur terrible retribution after death. With these fears, churches are able to hold their congregation in religious bias. For these converts and parishioners, this book offers a challenge and perhaps an escape through logic and reason to those minds that are pliable enough to explore or speculate on the history and the logic of religious beliefs.

If one were to make a bar graph comparing the progress and advances in science versus theology from the first century, the science bar would go off the chart, but theology would show no gain having been weighted down with the rejection of new ideas and its resultant ignorance. The theological bar needs to grow, and it is the purpose of this writing to attack that theological ignorance on the basis of logic and common sense.

A study of philosophy and the reading of the various theories of Lock, Hume, Barkley, Hobbs, Descartes and others in pondering the theories of good and evil, of life and death, reveal more questions than answers. When delving into religiosity, theocracy, theosophy, pantheism and other man-made, confining concepts, it would seem that religion should have to progress along with science in order to have a more compatible basis with the scientific truths.

From the time of Socrates to the present, philosophers, scientists and men of the cloth have presented ideas on what is ultimate reality. Less than 700 years ago there was a common perception that the world was flat. Today, it is common knowledge that the world is round, and obviously, that knowledge, not seen with the naked eye, is accepted as an unseen reality.

Space-age technology shows proof of that which the naked eye cannot see. This should indicate that eventually science will surpass religious beliefs that are based on mythology and reveal concepts that are based only on the qualities of truth.

We know that the science of mathematics and music can exist without a blackboard or musical instruments to express them; yet, it seems inconceivable to enjoy music without some form of materiality to see, feel, hear, or touch. The term "seems" is used because in our present, earth-born knowledge, we know nothing beyond matter except in the metaphysical fields as in music, mathematics and the sciences. Could there be another universe of infinite knowledge beyond our conception as an unseen reality? This writing will explore that concept.

Every error is an image of that which is true. In mathematics errors appear in numbers, in music--misapplied musical notes, a counterfeit dollar is an image of the real dollar; so is it beyond the realm of possibility that it could be hypothesized that the earth as it is now seen, is not a reality, but an image of a unseen reality?

Life on this earth presents enough confusion and enigmatical dilemmas for an argument that it is all one, big mistake. Whether or not one contemplates, the idea that there may be another reality to earth, the concept is worth considering. Presently, however, to expect mankind to view a new concept, other than matter as a true reality, might be compared to expecting a cave man to conceive of a computer program. This present knowledge was available to the cave man. Time does not increase, decrease, nor limit knowledge. The acquisition of knowledge may be stagnated by religions with their dogmatic ideas, and this may present a real contrast to science where new, hypothesized ideas are subject to an analysis and a challenge.

But eventually, knowledge will break through the fog of ignorance. It is the purpose of this writing to challenge the religious community to place their belief systems to a scientific analysis and tests of truth.

A religious concept that views God as a human, sows the seeds for vicious conflicts with other human gods who each have a different theology. One example of this is the concept that the Muslim Prophet Allah hates Christians, the followers of Jesus; thus, Islam extremists feel a justification in killing Christians.

The simple first step to diffuse this world problem of theological hate is to expose the fallacy of a humanized deity with the principles of logic and truth. As a beginning, this writing proposes logical, common sense arguments against Christian anthropomorphism.

If Christianity, the leading religion of the free world, is to lead the world in religious reformation, it should take a giant first step away from the current, religious, mythological concept that Jesus is God. According to the Christian Bible, Jesus corrected his followers in their attempt to worship him as God. He wanted to be considered the Messiah, not God. The dictionary defines the Messiah as a man., a leader, a deliverer who will deliver the Jewish people. In this regard, all the Christians need to do is follow their Bible.

INTRODUCTION

Ah love, could you and I with Him conspire
To grasp the Sorry Scheme of things entire
Would not we shatter it to bits, and then
Remold it nearer to the hearts desire?
Omar Khayyam

One of the pillars of a democratic society that could bring the world nearer hearts desire is education. An educated society may not be easily ruled by despots or dictators, but it may be misled by faulty teachings, as in the field of theology where, for example, the inquisition was fueled by beliefs in the reality of witchcraft and sorcery.

Presently, there is a movement by the Christian Right in the United States to destroy religious freedom by tearing down the wall that separates church and state. This is a wall that is the cornerstone of a democratic society, and it has its roots in the secular school system. To kill a tree, you destroy its roots. To destroy religious freedom, you destroy the secular school system.

As they read their Bible, the destruction of this school system is interpreted by the Christian Right as God's will. Unfortunately, over nine hundred years ago this same thinking process believed that killing witches was God's will.

It took from the 14th to the 18th century for Christians to realize that witches and witchcraft had no reality in truth. How many more centuries is it going to take before Christians realize that any concept of God must be based on rules of logic and must adhere to the qualities of truth.

It doesn't take a great theologian, or a learned scholar, to recognize that there is a great division in the King James Version of the Christian Holy Bible regarding the description and the operation of Deity. Isn't it possible that there were two distinct versions of God described in the manuscripts that the committee of churchmen used to compile the King James Version of the Bible? If the first two chapters of a text book give two versions of a controversial subject matter, could a logical assumption be made that one version would be presented as true, or in the case of conflict and indecision, both versions would be presented as true; thus, the decision for truth is left with the reader?

In this case, one version of Deity is that God is Love and Spirit. God's creation is only good as presented in the first chapter of Genesis. This is the God of Love, where all creatures live, move, and have their being as stated by St. Paul. In this version, God is Love. God is Spirit. On this side of the division, Jesus stated that "the Kingdom of God is within you." Evil in the form of Satan or Hell has no power, or real existence. In this version, Heaven and Hell are states of mind, and Satan is a lie that dissipates before the truth. Man has an innate, power of good over evil. Satan is a lie that attempts to destroy the power of truth.

In this first division, if God is defined as love and spirit in the Christian Bible, and it is assumed that the Christian Bible is used as the basis for the Christian theology, then the arguments set forth in this writing will be based on that theology. If both love and spirit are considered definitions of God, then it seems logical that many of the following congruent metaphysical entities could also apply to this definition. God could be considered the source of life, truth and intelligence. Additional terms for God that are congruent with spirit and love are: truth, immutability, omnipresence, purity, omniscience and omnipotence. Since some of these metaphysical entities presently exist in the daily lives of all living beings on the earth, the term "universal laws" were applied to them in this writing. As universal laws of good, they must also be attributes of God.

On the other side of the Bible's division, as stated in Genesis chapter II, is a God who thinks, acts like a mortal and is capable of great love, vengeance and hate. This is the God in the Garden of Eden who created the talking snake and the tree of evil fruit. He is the God who disenfranchised his first children of their perfect birthright. He is the God who commanded the slaughtering of the twelve thousand men, women and children of the Kingdom of Ai. The God of this version turned his first son into dust and another son into a pillar of salt. In this version, both God the Father and the God Jesus live in Heaven and only by Jesus' decision can one ascend from death to Heaven, or descend from death to Hell.

Today both versions of God are presented by the Christian clergy as biblical truths. Common sense should indicate otherwise. If purity and truth are attributes of God, then whatever version one has of God, that version cannot be a combination of opposites. God cannot be finite and infinite, temporal and eternal, unreal and real, mutable and immutable, evil and good, corporeal and incorporeal, the source of life and death, the source of love and hate. God cannot be both truth and error. Whatever is true about God, the opposite must be untrue. By comparing present-day theology to these over-simplified truths, it is obvious that today's concepts of God promulgated by the Christian clergy are not congruent with common sense logic or the attributes of truth. Isn't it time to challenge the veracity of this theology that has been accepted by millions of converts for over 2,000 years as truth?

Another difficult challenge will be for theists to set aside an ingrained bias, and place their own theological beliefs to the tests of logic and truth. It will be a more difficult challenge for the Christian clergy to give sermons based on the simplicity and purity of truth and set aside the fear of Satan as a reality opposed to Life, Love and Truth (God).

This writing will subject seven common mythologies to the test of truth. They are: Creationism, Heaven, Hell, Satan, the Trinity Concept, Jesus as God and Armageddon. These concepts are accepted by the majority of the Christian world as true, logical concepts, and as revealing the truth about God and His mode of operation. The concept of a humanized Deity is the most dangerous for world survival. An obvious example, is the Holy War the Islam extremists, the followers of Allah, have declared on the United States. When these religious extremists get the nuclear bomb, the days of the civilized world are numbered.

Yet in the face of this danger, the Christian clergy seem oblivious to this threat. They still promulgate Jesus as God as opposed to all the other dead-Man Gods of the world who may hate Jesus. What happened to the Christian concept of God as Love? How much hatred can be generated against the operation of Love?

If extremists succeed in their fanatic desire to explode atomic bombs in all the countries they perceive as enemies of Islam, they could ignite the destruction of Mother Earth into World War III. Isn't this a strange scenario for theists who hold religious beliefs based on an intelligent God who understands the importance of love?

Eventually, all governments must separate church rule from civil authority for the sake of world peace. In the writing of this book, the author presents a challenge to religious leaders to prove the veracity of their mythologies, as he questions the logic of their concepts, as well as the integrity of some of their policies.

CHAPTER I
CHRISTIAN MYTHOLOGIES

Religious beliefs differ in category from all other beliefs in that they are very personal and intimate and they expose one's belief system, but many are illogical, not based on fact. Children, whose beliefs represent a small minority, may learn from early childhood, and in school, how uncomfortable and embarrassing, or even how isolating it is, **not** to be part of the large majority's religious doctrine. Thus, religious schools give children surcease by offering commonality in beliefs.

Once in a comfortable belief system from childhood, the adult accepts the system as the truth without question. If this were not true, then there would not be millions of educated, religious converts genuflecting to mythological concepts. From the beginning of time, there has been very little common sense analysis applied to religious doctrine. In fact, it is almost unbelievable that educated adults in a technologically oriented society could not recognize the difference between a myth and a verifiable fact. For example, a very large segment of the Christian religion accepts a talking snake as factual, also, a Spirit that walks and talks to His two children in the Garden of Eden, or religious leaders who have communicated with their Man-God, or that man can be controlled by the Devil's demons, and so on.

Why must the belief in God be in the realm of mythology instead of a verifiable doctrine congruent with mathematics or scientific knowledge? Many Christian ministers are impervious to the oxymoron terms for God, as long as they can refute common sense logic by reciting biblical verses that substantiate their viewpoint. Eventually, people may demand more from religion than just setting ethical standards for a given society. In the meantime, the religious world will continue to genuflect to their Gods, and live in fear of Hell, Satan, and demons. Also, they accept without question present day concepts that defy logic such as Mary is the mother of God Jesus; thus making Jesus number two God. But Mary has no parents. Is God the Father and also the husband of Mary? God created Adam without a mother and yet He impregnated Mary to create Jesus. Why the difference? Can there be creation without a female? Does Mary have two husbands—God and Joseph? Does God need a female to create life? If begotten means to procreate, how could Jesus be God's only begotten son when Adam and Eve created Able and Cain, but Jesus, the begotten son, had no offspring?

If these myths were written in a child's fairy-tale book, there would be no controversy regarding their authenticity. The talking snake would have the same veracity as the talking wolf in Little Miss Riding Hood and Satan would have the same power as the evil giant in Jack in the Bean-stalk

Are the Christian Churches in the world still promulgating mythology? Does this indicate that after 2000 years of teaching Christianity that this religion is based more on mythology than on verifiable truth? See the article on exorcism in the Seattle Times, February 13, 2004. The article stated that by a popular request from a small town in Italy, some Christian religious leaders made a present-day search for the Devil's use of Demons. It is quite shocking that in the educated world of the 21st century, that there still exists a strong belief in Satan, as a deadly enemy of God. And that some day in the future, God will fight the war of Armageddon with Satan and kill him. Then all evil will be destroyed and there will be peace in the world. (And we all will live happily ever-after.) Is this war really logical? Does it take the act of killing to give the world eternal life and peace? Thus, making the death of Satan a final act of God for a utopian life for all Christians!

The myths presented in the following chapters seem to be common to present-day religions:

THE GARDEN OF EDEN

The following verses are excerpts taken from the book of Genesis chapters one, two, and three in the King James Version of the Holy Bible.

These verses cover the salient points in the allegory of Adam and Eve in the Garden of Eden.

CREATIONISM BEGINNING WITH GENESIS

GENESIS CHAPTER I

Genesis 1:1, 27, 31.

1. In the beginning God created the heaven and earth.

27. So God created man in his own image, in the image of God created he him; male and female created he them.

31. And God saw everything that he had made, and behold it was very good. And the evening and the morning were the sixth day.

GENESIS CHAPTER II

Genesis 7, 18, 22.

7. And the Lord God formed man of the dust of the ground and breathed into his nostrils the breath of life; and man became a living soul.

18. And the Lord God said, It is not good that man should be alone; I will make him a help meet for him.

22. And the rib which the lord God had taken from man, made he woman , and brought her unto man.

GENESIS CHAPTER III

Genesis 3: 1, 2, 3, 4, 5, 6, 13, 16. 20, 22, 23, 2.4.

1. Now the serpent was more subtle than any beast of the field which the Lord had made. And he said unto woman, Yea, hath God said Ye shall not eat of every tree of the garden.

2. And the women said unto the serpent, "We may eat of the fruit of every tree of the garden."

3. "But of the fruit of the tree which is in the midst of the garden, God hath said Ye shall not eat of, neither shall ye touch it, lest ye die."

4. And the serpent said unto the woman, Ye shall not surely die.

5. For God doth know that in the day ye eat thereof, then your eyes will be opened and ye shall be as Gods, knowing good and evil.

6. And when the woman saw that the tree was good for food, and it was pleasant to the eyes, and a tree to be desired and make one wise, she took of the fruit thereof, and did eat, and gave unto her husband with her and he did eat.

8. And they heard the voice of the Lord walking in the garden in the cool of the day and they hid themselves from the presence of the Lord.

13. And the Lord said unto woman, "What is this that thou hast done?" And the woman said, "The serpent beguiled me and I did eat."

16. Unto the women he said, "I will greatly multiply thy sorrow and thy conception; in sorrow thou shalt bring forth children; and thy desire shall be to thy husband and he shall rule over thee."

17. And unto Adam he said, "Because thou hast hearkened unto the voice of thy wife and hast eaten from the tree of which I commanded thee saying thou shalt not eat of: cursed is the ground for thy sake; and in sorrow shalt thou eat of it all the days of thy life."

20. And Adam called his wife's name Eve; because she was the mother of all living.

22. And the Lord God said, "Behold, man has come as one of us to know good and evil: and now lest he put forth his hand, and take of the tree of life, and eat, and live for ever."

23. Therefore the Lord God sent him forth from the Garden of Eden to till the ground from whence he was taken.

24. So he drove out the man; and he placed at the east of the Garden of Eden Cherubims and a flaming sword which turned everyway, to keep the way of the tree of life.

THE GARDEN OF EDEN, FACT OR FICTION

Those Christians who view Creationism as depicted in the book of Genesis as a factual event, depart from logical cogency in favor of mind-stunted fanaticism. No credence is given by Christian Fundamentalists to thinkers who demand conviction by evidence rather than blind, slavish, worship of an illogical dogma. The thinking members of the Christian World must realize that Christian theology must have its roots placed in verifiable evidence of truth and not in an illogical fable.

THE DICHOTOMY PERSISTS

In effort to free those minds that are imprisoned in the rigid armor of doctrine, the following inconsistencies in Creationism are presented for cogitation:

1. The Christian Bible is used as a book of religious instruction in many Christian churches. It begins with the second chapter contradicting the first chapter, and it ends with the ideology of the New Testament contradicting the ideology of the Old Testament. Is it logical that a biblical account of a God, whose actions are good, is also described as a God whose actions are evil?

2. The first chapter of Genesis states that God's creation is wholly good. This included the world and all living creatures in it, both male and female.

Abruptly, the second chapter refutes the first chapter by stating that there was evil in the form of a tree in the midst of the Garden of Eden. Where did all this evil come from? Which was first the tree or Adam? It is obvious by this story that the tree was first. Regardless of the time frame involved, evil (sin) had to be available before Eve tasted the apple. So how could she or Adam be blamed for all the sin in the world? If the Christian God created the Garden of Eden, God must be responsible for the evil tree in the midst of the garden. Was all the evil in the world confined to a fruit tree until Eve ate the apple? How did Adam by digesting an apple release all the evil in the world unless his Father, God, released it? God was in control of it. Do rational thinking Christians believe this story as a factual event? To believe this story, the reader must acknowledge that God, the creator of good, is also a God, the creator of evil. The Christian God, then, becomes an operational contradiction.

5

3. Christians think of God and His creation as eternal. The first chapter of Genesis starts with the words "In the beginning." Eternity has no beginning! Therefore, the story of Adam and Eve in the Garden of Eden must be an allegory. This story has a benign beginning and a disastrous ending which is not congruous with an eternal God of Love and Intelligence. Is it logical that an eternal, omnipotent, all intelligent, God would create such an evil, chaotic, temporal creation? In reading the book of Genesis, a reasonable question to ask is which is true all the attributes of a good God, or the book of Genesis?

4. Immutability must be an attribute of truth and God. Creationism defies and denies that quality in the vicissitudes of fantasy. Why would a rational God of good create an evil, talking serpent with more knowledge than man?

Then why did God take away that snake's intelligence because he used his intelligence as God knew he would? Doesn't this God know the future as well as the present? The Bible states that God created in Eden a fruit tree with fruit of evil knowledge. None of these entities has a record of a viable existence outside of fantasy.

5. The equanimity of the Christian God in Genesis, chapter one, becomes a disturbed, irritated, vengeful, hostile God in the other chapters of Genesis. Which God is the real, true immutable God?

6. The Christian God of the infinite Holy Spirit became a finite, mortal-like God walking and talking in the Garden of Eden seeking evidence for retribution. Can the infinite be encased in the finite? Is there revenge in Love? God is Love! The God of Jesus says, "Turn the other cheek."

7. Is it logical for a God who knows the past, present and future, and who is the loving parent of Adam and Eve, to devise such a diabolical scheme of entrapment for Eve? Her encounter with the talking snake ostracized her forever from her father's presence. Since God knew the outcome of this encounter before He set it in motion, doesn't this action defy common sense for a loving Father?

8. Many theologians will argue that God gave Adam a "free will" in order to make decisions; therefore, God could not interfere with Adam's decision to defy him. This argument treats free will as some sort of involuntary force that is separate from one's life and intelligence. "Free will" requires

life and intelligence to make a decision; so with this premise, it requires God to make a decision against Himself. How, then, could "free will" separate man from God when no decision can be made without life and intelligence--the source of which are God's attributes? Thus, this so-called schism between God and man that is supposedly created by "free will," must be an impossibility. The schism concept is presently promulgated by Christian Fundamentalists as factual!

9. Regarding the snake, has anyone ever asked why the snake chose to talk to Eve instead of Adam? Adam was the man in charge. Or was the snake a typical male chauvinist who would rather talk to a nude lady. And then, there is this creation thing. What loving parent would choose to create a snake with more intelligence than his son and daughter, and then use its intelligence to destroy his loving relationship with His offspring? Does any Christian believe this about their God? A God that is only Love!

Doesn't this allegory demonstrate the Bible's male orientation where a woman is totally to blame, not only for disobedience to God, but also for the downfall of Adam? Is this a hidden message that without the creation of woman, this would have been a perfect world? It seems to be the Christian view that woman was punished and made inferior to man for eating the forbidden fruit and sharing it with her mate.

10. After Eve's indiscretion, God became so angry he talked man to man with Adam. Today, there are many atrocities and horrors taking place all over God's world. Why isn't God talking man to man to world leaders who are destroying His world? The answer must be that there never was an Adam and Eve, or a God who talks. If God is equated with intelligence, intelligent communication comes in ideas and the ability to express them and not in oral words spoken from a Man-God.

11. The Christians refer to their God as monotheistic; yet they accept the term Gods as used throughout the chapters of Genesis as the truth e.g. (Genesis 3: 5, 22...) and ye shall be as Gods. And the Lord God said, "Behold, man has become one of us." The use of the word "us" in this case refers to multiple Gods. How can Christians believe their God is monotheistic and still believe in Genesis? The Christian God must be either monotheistic or polytheistic. It cannot be both.

12. Also, in verse 22, life is portrayed by the Gods in the book of Genesis as both eternal and temporal. Which is true? If one could eat of the Tree

of Life, life would be eternal. Otherwise, it states life is temporal. Is that logical? If the life in the Tree of Life is eternal, where and what is the source of temporal life? Are there two sources of life? It should be obvious this part of the allegory doesn't make much sense.

13. In this allegory Adam was created from dust and Eve was created from Adam's rib. As the first male and female created by God, they became man and wife. Eve was created from Adam; so Eve had Adam's genes, and both Adam and Eve had the same father; therefore, they were also brother and sister. Couldn't this make their children the result of what is now termed incest?

14. The enigmatic premise of the Trinity gives additional lineage in the allegory of Creationism. In terms of eternity, time is finite, a temporal measurement; therefore, in eternity there is no time. Jesus as one third of the Trinity is an eternal God. God created Adam; thus Jesus as God, is Adam's father. As the son of God, Jesus is also Adam's brother. Does this relationship make sense? Can a man be both father and brother to his own offspring?

Does it make sense for a loving father to let one son die and give eternal life to another son? If God is the source of eternal life, how could Adam's life be temporal and Jesus' life eternal? Is God an inconsistent source of life? If there is life after death, Adam must be either in Heaven or Hell; unless returning to dust or salt are the other options after death for sinners and all non-Christians?

15. In this Genesis Creation, Adam returned to dust. If Jesus' resurrection proved life to be indestructible, and if Adam ever lived, wouldn't his life also be indestructible and not subject to the ignominy of dust? How could God create for the purpose of damnation? If God is the whole of life, how can a part of life (Adam) be removed from life? Isn't the whole the sum of its parts?

16. It was Adam who ate the apple that caused all the sin in the world. So why did God let mortals nail his brother, Jesus, to the cross for Adam's sin? Why didn't God let mortals nail Adam to the cross to expiate for mankind's sins? It certainly seems that would be more in the line of justice. Why did Jesus have to pay for his brother's mistake? Or is Adam his son? The Bible is not very clear in regard to that relationship.

17.   Genesis 3: 16. Woman was created to be a help-meet for Adam, and she is to be ruled by Adam. Would a loving father want his daughter to become a slave to her husband?   In this allegory woman was inferior to man. (A time-worn Christian concept) As one who is responsible for propagating the race, the female is truly the equal if not the superior of the sexes. And what male in his right mind, living in a free society, would dare declare himself superior to his wife and then expect to receive and enjoy all the nuptial benefits?

18.   There are at least 60 million Catholics and 30 million Protestants who believe that all mortals created by God are sinners, but all of them will have eternal life after death either in Heaven or Hell. Are all these Christians (ex-sinners) in Heaven better than Adam? Doesn't this belief conflict with the story of Adam who died and was returned to dust? Again, how could the immutable source of eternal life destroy life?

19.   Christians believe, as stated in the book of Genesis, that God created the universe without evolution.   Astronomers report that the universe is constantly expanding and creating planets and galaxies. How could an immutable Creator change his mind and now create our present universe with an evolutionary process?

20. If the Christian concept of one God as the source of eternal life and love is accepted as the truth, then it is obvious that the book of Genesis does not present Creationism as the truth.

21.God's world was perfect without sin, or death. Then Eve ate the apple in this perfect world, and committed a sin. She sinned before it was possible to sin. Is this logical?

22 There are states that are promoting the allegory of "Creationism" in their public schools as the true words from God--a violation of our First Amendment. How could educated parents want this allegory to be taught as factual to their children, and not realize the deleterious affect it would have on their children's ability to think clearly and not accept fantasy as truth?

23. The term "Intelligent Design is a new term for "Creationism". As a term for true Creation it is still illogical and mythological.   Biblical Creationism presents and depicts God as a dichotomy. In the Christian Bible Spirit and Love are terms for God. Would an intelligent Eternal

Supreme Being create a temporal, material world subject to chaos and violence? And also create intricate material bodies that are subject to sickness, horrible diseases and death and call it intelligent design? Is this the best logic the Christian right can promulgate?

Surely to teach the world about God there should be some sort of common sense logic based on qualities of truth. Shouldn't the theology of Jesus have a basis in qualities of truth?

The United States is facing very dangerous times. Weapons of mass destruction can be carried in a briefcase by any zealot who believes Allah wants our nation destroyed. Do Christians believe that Allah is a prophet of a mythological God? If so, is there proof? Muslims believe that Allah has the same viable existence as the Christian prophet Jesus. Can Christians prove them wrong?

More than any time in the past, our nation must have leaders who are aware that the new technological age is making the world smaller through communication. People with different mores and religious beliefs must learn to live and work together. Our nation's leaders must be globally oriented, tolerant, devoid of religious bias, and have the sagacity to defuse confrontations between followers of mythological entities with strong and diverse ideological beliefs. There is an urgent need for all the Christian people to have an important role in expanding the depolarization of religious education. Education must become more universal and denounce all forms of anthropomorphism that cause religious wars and the polarization of religious beliefs.

Will Christianity, the religion of the free world, be up to the task? Not very likely! With the Catholic world genuflecting to the Pope, the Protestant world worshiping Jesus, and the Muslims world bowing to their God, it seems it is more realistic to expect Christians to defend Christian mythology as the truth, send all non-believers to Hell, and kill all Muslims before the Muslims kill all Christians. And so world strife continues. Let us hope that this view can be modified with a perceived need for universal love without religious mandates between all nations.

THE TRINITY ANALYZED

The Apostles' Creed gives the three-person-in-one concept of God which is known as the Trinity. The majority, but not all Christian churches, subscribe to this concept of God. Those who believe in this concept deny that it is a polytheistic view of one Christian God.

The Apostles' Creed begins with: I BELIEVE IN GOD THE FATHER ALMIGHTY MAKER OF HEAVEN AND EARTH, AND JESUS CHRIST, HIS ONLY (BEGOTTEN) SON, OF OUR LORD WHO WAS CONCEIVED BY THE HOLY SPIRIT, BORN OF THE VIRGIN MARY.

I BELIEVE IN THE HOLY SPIRIT.

These three beliefs in God, the Father, Jesus His Son and the Holy Spirit comprise the Trinity concept of God. It is very difficult for a non-Christian to conceive of a father and son to be one entity when they are stated as two entities in the Creed. The Father is designated as the creator of Heaven and earth, and Jesus, His son, is designated as the son of the creator who is a separate entity from the creator.

The Holy Spirit, also called the Holy Ghost, is viewed by some Christians as a Holy Person or an amorphous concept of Jesus' body after his resurrection. It is not possible for a father and son to be one entity here on earth; so how is it possible in Heaven? Many Christians pray to Jesus as God. This in essence makes Jesus his own creator and father, with his dead body as the concept of the Holy Ghost ascending to Heaven. Whatever type of thinking is responsible for this concept, it certainly obscures the simplicity of the biblical teaching which states there is only one God, Spirit.

The Trinity concept was conceived very early in the Christian Church and received much amplification in the First Ecumenical Council. The usual statement of the doctrine is that "God exists in three persons all coequal and indivisible of the same substance--God the Father, God the son, (who became incarnate as Jesus) begotten of the Father God and the Holy Ghost preceding from the Father and the Son. The Trinity is considered by most Christian teachers to be a mystery; its nature cannot be fully understood by human intelligence. It is, therefore, called truth by revelation; however, if the Trinity is beyond human intelligence, where is the revelation? Was

11

it revealed only to the people who conceived of it? If the Trinity is the truth of God, wouldn't He want it revealed logically without a mysterious flaw? A flaw that portrays God as both corporeal and incorporeal--two opposites! This mystery is commemorated liturgically in the western churches on Trinity Sunday.

By its very definition, "incarnate" precludes God as being the immutable, Holy Spirit. Incarnate is the opposite of Spirit. Trinity is a concept of one spiritual, infinite God circumscribed into three diverse entities. There are two humanized entities, assuming the Father and the son are of the same substance, and one amorphous entity, the Holy Spirit conceived as one God. This concept defies logic. One God comprised of two substances (spirit and body) needs two thrones for one entity. God must be a term for immutable truth. How can two men, with mortal bodies become one immutable, infinite, spiritual God? How does one conceive of one Spirit in the form of two men and a Holy Spirit?

It is possible that the early Christians, who conceived of the Trinity concept, recognized the incongruity of its definition; so they covered it with the words: "beyond human intelligence." This, evidently, made it easy for the early Christian world to accept the Trinity as God without question. However, God cannot be a combination of two opposing substances that are both temporal and eternal. The Bible states that God is Spirit. The Trinity designates God as two magnified, material mortals and one spiritual entity; thus with this description God becomes an oxymoron.

Christianity was founded on the life of a man called Jesus with his healing works and his teachings. He is viewed in the Christian Bible as one man, the Messiah. The Trinity views Jesus as God. This concept seems to give Christians a personification of the amorphous entities of Spirit, Life, Love, Intelligence and Truth. The Trinity views Jesus and his Father as two mortal concepts with mortal propensities. By definition the Trinity is not homogenous. The Holy Spirit is different in nature from God, the Father and God, the Son. "Different in nature" divides the Trinity which is considered indivisible. Thus, the Trinity cannot be truth, because truth cannot be subject to change. Different indicates a change, a divergence. Truth is constant and immutable. How can Jesus, a corporeal man, be God, if God is immutable spirit? Unless, of course, God is not Spirit as it is stated in the Bible.

The Bible refers to truth as an attribute of God. Truth cannot be a separate entity from God. Truth and God must be one. Truth cannot change from amorphous to incarnate, or corporeal and incorporeal and still be truth. Therefore, the Trinity has no basis in truth!

HEAVEN AND HELL ANALYZED

The sum of all thoughts can be measured in terms of how successful their metaphysical capabilities can control the physical aspects in life. The extent of this control determines the quality of the life that is lived. One erroneous measuring rod for the success of this control is personal wealth which controls all facets of poverty and leisure time. The true measuring rod is in the realm of metaphysical dominion over all facets of materialism. The power of material forces in the world and in the universe, is awesome; yet, astrophysicists have calculated the complete self-destruction of these forces.

For example, the late Doctor Sagan and his associates stated the premise that the earth was formed by a huge cosmic cloud that was ten to twenty light years in diameter swirling in space. Within this cloud heavy particles of dust began developing gravitational fields that over a 100 million years grew like a huge snowball dragging into it gas and minerals within its core to form our planet earth and other planets, suns and solar systems.

The astrophysicists believe that there are millions of planets in these clouds in all stages of development from being born to dying of old age. There are large galaxies swallowing smaller galaxies and black holes swallowing all galaxies. Sooner or later the earth may be compressed into the size of a basketball and then further compressed into gas as it exits a black hole.

Eventually the energy in the universe will be depleted or transformed and the universe will no longer exist in a physical state.

The difference between the metaphysical and physical qualities within the universe denotes the problem of true entity. Do these different qualities comprise one entity in matter or two? If one, they both die in matter by self destruction, because one entity could not exist without the other (such as life in a material body). As separate entities, the metaphysical entity is self-existent, indestructible and harmonious. In daily life we experience all forms of material substance that through the ravages of time are on the road to complete annihilation.

In assuming two entities the problem presented to the astrophysicists is the origin of the physical entities. Dr. Sagan and his associates developed the premise that the material universe began with nothing and ultimately will end with nothing. This seems to validate the findings so far of the Quantum Mechanics string theory that found no origin of matter. These findings may confirm the theory that if the ultimate reality in the universe is metaphysical, then its opposite the physical, has no reality which obviously includes all matter in the swirling cloud.

At present, however, there is reason to believe that there is life on many of the planets in these clouds. The French Scientists hypothesize that Unidentified Flying Objects (UFO's) come from a planet 14 light-years from earth. The United States Government denies that UFOs exist. If Church leaders might speculate that there is Heaven or Hell on one of these clouds, their origin could deny their belief in "Creationism." To date the Darwin theory of evolution has more creditability among astrophysicists than does the Christian Bible's explanation of creation. These are examples that prove when there are diversities of beliefs, myths may assume authenticity, because there is no incontrovertible, verifiable evidence that Heaven and Hell do not exist. If it is assumed that they exist in material state, then as matter they have no verifiable origin or existence. They must self-destruct with the universe. If it is assumed that they exist as metaphysical entities, then Heaven would take on the attributes of good (God) only, and as a concept of evil, Hell will self-destruct and become nothing as do errors in mathematics.

There are as many concepts of Heaven as there are creeds. For the Muslims, Heaven is a place without Christians--a very dangerous place for Christians. For the American Indian, Heaven is a happy hunting ground--a bad place for the animal activist. For the "born-again" Christian, Heaven is a utopian plane where non-believers in Jesus are excluded. For the Christian Scientist, Heaven is a state of mind--no one excluded. For Jehovah Witnesses, Heaven is the earth transformed into a paradise--and so on and so on.

No living mortal knows what lies beyond death. Probably to make the horror of death more palatable to Christian thought, Christians give death a silver lining called a trip to Heaven--the abode of God with all of the worshippers living on a utopian plane of purity and perfection with Jesus. However, the only road to this Heaven is death. Logically, if there is a Heaven, wouldn't the road to it be alive with God's beauty, rather than with disease, sickness and dead bodies? Beyond this belief in Heaven, lies the ugly truth of logic and common sense that death is not preferable to life.

Death is a negative--not a positive. It is the end result of a terrible tragedy, the termination of a fatal sickness, disease, or the end of the aging process and the unavoidable termination of many happy lives. It is the direct opposite of life and its source. To be alive promotes growth, both physical and mental. Death terminates that growth. Logically then, how could death immediately change from a negative to a positive and become man's most positive experience in life--a sudden transfer to a utopian plane called Heaven. Jesus said, "The kingdom of God is within you." (Luke 17:21) How do Christian leaders reconcile promulgating Heaven as a physical locality against this statement of Jesus--the man they consider to be their God?

The concept of a continuous life must also preclude the concept of Heaven as an existent reality on the basis that the present life is the future of a past life before birth. So, how do Christian leaders, who are so positive of Heaven in the hereafter, ever explain to their congregations: (1) this unavoidable concept must relate to a past life, and (2) how does God solve all the conflicting ramifications of life in Heaven? For example: How does a mother, whose son died at childbirth, recognize her mature son in Heaven? Does the memory of life go with the departed? If so, then the composite memory of life in Heaven would be the same as on earth-- anything but pure.

Consider the man who lost his wife six months after their marriage, married again and lived to become became a grandfather. Was it fair that God let this young wife suffer sadness in Heaven while her husband was married to another woman on earth? Finally when the husband enters Heaven, he now has two wives who want to continue their marriage. What does he do? Is polygamy allowed in Heaven? Do those wives want to share their husband?

If there are the young, married couples who want children, what do they do? If life is eternal, without beginning or ending, there can be no birth or death. If all who live in Heaven are in the prime of life, how can there

15

be children? Do murdered children as well as those who died from other causes appear in Heaven as adults? Without birth would there be a need for sexual differences?

Is there justice? For example, a man who embezzled and bankrupted his boss and then became a born-again Christian. The boss murdered his family to save them the shame of poverty. This family is now living in Heaven, and they miss their father, the boss, who is suffering eternal damnation in Hell without reprieve. Is this justice?

With billions of people in Heaven, there would be billions of problems to solve. Heaven would be as problematic as earth. Do Christian leaders have logical answers to give to their congregations other than quoting some verse from the Bible?

If Heaven represents a state of perfection, then the lowly "born-again" Christian who dies in a state of imperfection (a sinner) would find no solace in Heaven. Isn't it reasonable to suggest that the imperfect would have to gain a state of perfection before reaching Heaven? Otherwise, Heaven and Heavenly thinking for this Christian would be his Hell. He wouldn't fit! The more one contemplates Heaven after death, the more illogical it becomes.

Before death, any Christian who purports to attain in his lifetime the mentality of heavenly perfection, would be ushered to the nearest mental institution. However, if that same person believes he could have that Heavenly perfection immediately after his death, he would be considered a normal, "born-again" Christian. How wonderful is this death process for Christians! They view death as a judgment time for Jesus to intercede with God on their behalf for a place in Heaven. Will he or won't he? This is the great fear. Only good Christians will be chosen. Isn't any view of the hereafter strictly a human speculation that is not based on factual evidence? Though the whole Christian world believes in Heaven that does not make it factual!

Suppose the scientific community were to develop a method to eliminate death--the road to Heaven. The world population of Christians would have to overcome problems of racism, nationalism, hatred, violence, sin, sickness, and disease right here on earth. Once in Heaven, God would have handled those problems. Yet without death, how does one get to

Heaven? Is one solution to this scenario--go back to church and pray for the return of death as the true road to Heaven?

HELL

Success in life is measured in terms of progress and in overcoming great odds. The greater odds--the greater is the progress. Many times failures in life have led to the greatest of triumphs in learning and molding strength of character. By making mistakes, man learns what is right, and what is wrong. It is through the dissatisfaction of wrong doing that one is led back to the operation of good.

Adhering to the laws of love, integrity, justice and goodness in relationships with others are good laws of conduct for all mankind. This may take more than a lifetime for some mortals to learn, because of the circumstances and environment in which they are raised on earth. After death, are they going to be condemned to Hell because of the wrong mental concepts that they were taught as the truth?

Sometimes men select hatred, dishonesty, selfishness and evil as their conduct of choice. Examples of this, are the lives of the pre-war leaders of Iraq. Sometimes this type of conduct produces temporary wealth, but most of the time it leads to failures and self destruction or imprisonment. At the most, it produces dissatisfaction and unpopular accomplishments that may cause the perpetrators to change their ways. In some cases, people have turned away from negative thinking and have become better people than others who never took the low road.

According to most traditional religious doctrines, there are three well-established concepts of life after death. (1) There is a place called Heaven where God and Jesus reside. (2) There is a place called Hell ruled by Satan. (3) After death, people will have eternal life in either Heaven or Hell.

On earth, Hell is for women trapped under Muslim religious rule. Hell is for African women suffering sexual mutilation under religious rule. Hell is for victims of terrorists; Hell is for victims of torture. Life is Hell for all poverty-stricken third world residents living on garbage dumps. Hell is found in many world prisons with their torture chambers. Could Satan's Hell be any worse?

Satan's Hell is eternal. It captures all non-believers of Muslim theology including all Christians with no possible escape. Victims are there as the result of believing in the wrong God. Satan rules! He allows no help, no education, no reform, no correction of wrongs, no change of thought, and he assures eternal damnation, punishment and torture.

Earth's Hell, like Satan's Hell, is in many places the result of believing in the wrong God. But there are eleemosynary institutions attempting to eliminate earth's Hell in poverty through acts of charity. In prisons there are parole boards to encourage and reward positive behavior. There is a slow movement worldwide to recognize individual rights. So all in all, Satan's Hell is worse than earth's Hell with but one great exception. There is positively and absolutely no evidence what-so-ever, that Satan's Hell exists.

So if the belief in Hell is like a mathematical error with no principle in truth, it will self-destruct. Then won't all errors, regardless of kind, also self-destruct? Hell must self-destruct and cease to exist because it is the opposite of the fundamental principle of good. Jesus referred to Satan as a liar. The lie has no principle in truth for its existence. If truth and good are realities, then their opposites have to be unrealities.

The question often asked, "Is how does an omnipotent, good God allow so much Hell on earth?" The answer must be that God is not a man with eyes that see. Rather, God is a term for the laws of good that operate as efficaciously as do the laws and principles of mathematics for the mathematician working a math problem. The solution of the problem is in the principle of mathematics. It is up to the mathematician to find it and apply it. For the principle of good to exist, it must be ever present. The starving families living on garbage dumps must realize that the knowledge to get off the garbage dump is present. It is necessary for those going through Hell on the dump to find it.

The Bible gave the example of Paul in prison. His chains dropped off and the prison doors opened and he walked out. Whether this story is factual or not, it does open the door to the possibility of positive thought. There are positive forces on earth moving toward saving the world environment and preserving individual freedoms, but overcoming negative forces is a very slow process. If the power of good is able to operate with positive results on earth, why is it inconceivable that they could not operate after death in Satan's Hell? Where in the universe is anyone prevented from a change of thought? So, again, how could Hell exist as an eternal entity, or until the battle of Armageddon?

What mortal was told by God that He elected only a few good Christians to enter Heaven with the remainder of his creation going to Hell? Isn't good available to all men? Why would the immutable, all inclusive good laws of Love, Life, and Intelligence become exclusive and selective? These laws are available to all humans and it is imperative that humans learn to utilize them. Man was given the gifts of life, love, intelligence and the environment for his care. His lack of appreciation for the latter is obvious. Hopefully his wanton destruction of wildlife and the environment will be replaced with the power of love.

How could evil, the Devil, or Satan exist in a place where the laws of good do not exist? Are there laws of evil that can overpower good? Or is evil the absence of good? There are many theists who believe in the power of evil or Satan that can destroy the power of good. "As a man thinketh so is he." There is certainly evidence of tremendous evil in the world; however, there is also overwhelming evidence of good. Whichever is dominant is directly proportional to the power behind the thinking of the individual or the composite thinking of a group that believes in it. It should be obvious that any entity that lacks a positive, principle of good must also lack ultimate reality. If the Christian Fundamentalist believes in the negative power of evil or Satan, but he also acknowledges the positive power of God, he is like the man in Jesus' parable who tries to serve two masters. If he makes a reality of both, he will fear both. He will eventually love one and hate the other. If his allegiance is to God, that allegiance would be vitiated by his fear and his belief in the reality of another power opposed to his omnipotent God.

There are now six billion people on our planet. Fewer than 25% are Christians. If one should estimate how many people in the past, the present and future will live in Hell, Hell is going to be a very overcrowded place. To lose all these offspring, must be a real tragedy for the Christian God as well as for the Muslim God. Isn't it logical that these all powerful men-Gods would have long ago changed the status quo to prevent this from happening? If the Bible states that the kingdom of God is a state of thought, isn't it possible that biblical references to Hell could also be a state of thought?

To believe otherwise, confronts the following beliefs of the Satanic Cult:

19

1. The omnipresence of good is not present in Hell. For this to happen, God and Satan would be two man-Gods making a pact to betray a vast creation.

2. Mistakes do not self-destruct, but have a cause base in the Devil. According to Satan believers, lies, ignorance, errors, and evil would have a permanent reality and would not allow intelligence, life, love to exist.

3. Satan's forgiveness is not possible in Hell. All mistakes are personified and punished forever. The belief in Hell is the thought that a negative force of evil is a force that will destroy the positive force of good.

4. Satan's evil is a reality that believers think will destroy everything that is good, because there can not be an opposite reality to evil.

All the above are some of the beliefs of the Satanic Cult. Doesn't the sincere Christian, who accepts Satan as a reality, unwittingly become a member in thought with the Satanic Cult and give credence to the Cult's beliefs? And doesn't Christianity, the religion of the free world, embrace the Satanic Cult as part of its theology by promulgating Satan as a living reality that God must eventually destroy?

Does the intransigent, mob mentality of the general Christian population accept the validity of Heaven and Hell to the point of death? Is it possible that in the "Sorry Scheme of Things" that only through a death and a rebirth process, that this intransigent mentality of mythological convictions could be moved to a cogent thinking level?

Finally, isn't the concept of Satan and Hell an origination of Islam, and in the Christian religions a method used to explain the causes for misfortunes, tragedies and death? It is also a means of instilling fear in those who veer from normally accepted behavior and mores of an accepted society, and its common beliefs.

For 2000 years, Christians have been convinced that Heaven and Hell exist. Now, to change the validity and location of those concepts may cause such confusion that it could take another 2000 years for Christian leaders to accept the logic of a non-existent Heaven and Hell. Consider for a moment that if the concept of Heaven and Hell were no longer a part of the Christian ministry, sermons would be no longer concerned about Jesus' role in death and its afterlife, or God's forgiveness of sin. This would cause drastic changes in the Christian view of death, life, Jesus and sin. Let us hope that Christians may, at least, consider the lack of logic and validity in these old, time-worn, mythological concepts. Religion devoid of mythology could bring a new dawn in the millennium.

CHAPTER II

PROBLEMATIC CONCEPTS

A PARTIAL SURVEY OF THE
CHRISTIAN CHURCHES' POPULATION
IN THE MILLIONS AS OF 1998

United Methodist	8.5
Episcopal	2.3
Roman Catholic	60.2
Jehovah's Witness	1.0
Southern Baptist	<u>16.0</u>
Total	88.0

The Seattle Post Intelligencer, April 17, 2000. Section D Page 6

It is obvious that not all protestant sects are represented in the above census, but it does give the extent of the consensus of Christian theology with its mythology.

A SHORT SKETCH
OF THE PROBLEMS AND TRAGEDIES CAUSED BY
RELIGIOUS BELIEFS

THE WORST OF CHRISTIANITY

At the present time there are over 90 million Christians in the world who are church members. Isn't it strange that there has not been one among them who is able to emulate the works of Jesus, their teacher?

With all these Christians around the world, one wonders why there isn't more promotion of Jesus' theology doctrine of love. The conflict between two religious factions in Kosovo gave the United Nation's peace keepers a battle for peace. Some Christian Churches have recently come under attack as breeding grounds for past and present activities of pedophilic priests whose sexual proclivities seem to outweigh piousness. Is there a morality void in these religious organizations that supposedly promote love, morality and family values? After 2,000 years of Christianity, is there now less hatred, violence, and immorality in the world? Is it possible that the true, powerful theology of original Christianity has been lost by those church leaders who misinterpret the scripture and equate ritual, mundane power, riches, numbers of converts and the resulting prestige as the will of God?

On March 22, 2004, Sheik Ahmed Yassin was killed by an Israeli missile fired from an Israeli helicopter as he left the Mosque. Tens of thousands of Gaza residents, some with tears in their eyes, poured into the streets blaming Israel and the United States for his death. Some political pundits of Middle East politics state that his assassination does more harm than good. Killing generates more hatred and violence than acts of love for peace. It also places the United States in danger for more terrorists' attacks from a united Arab World. The Bush administration countered with the statement, "Israel has the right to defend itself."

Presently, in the United States there is an attack by the Religious Right on the First Amendment of the Constitution. They want their religious concepts taught in all of the nation's schools. For the sake of an argument, let us assume that religious education would be required in all schools. Immediately we would be faced with the following questions: which religious subject matter would be taught? Who will make that decision? How does congress distribute funds to the churches for education? The power, prestige and influence of the church depend on the flow of money. How would minority churches receive equal representation for funds and proselytizing for their schools? Could there be unanimity in congress for the distribution of religious funds? But would there be laws to protect the rights of minority churches and non-Christian education? Would there be enough wealth to support the multitude of church-school systems? If not, who would decide which schools could survive?

It is not difficult to imagine the uprisings and internal strife that would result from a policy of combining church power with the state. The diversity in religious doctrine is the basis of all the religious wars. Where there is no freedom of religion, there is no freedom from religion. Iran is a good example of the problems of unrest incurred with church-state rule when there is only one dominate religion. Multiply their problems by the number of different dominations existing in the United States. The enormity and complexities of the problems of church-state rule would be overwhelming and certainly would become more apparent by observing the religious strife worldwide. Observe the violence generated between the Shiites and Sunni Muslims in the Middle East.

There are over 90 million Christians donating billions of dollars annually to support church growth. To this figure add the value worldwide of all the church lands, buildings, robes for pageantry, books and church furnishings. Add to this, the cost of wars in fighting or competing with other factions in both present and past centuries. Consider the Christian churches in the third world with their magnificent golden edifices in the poorest of villages amid crumbling shacks inhabited by a pitiful, poverty stricken, starving populace that nevertheless, still tithe from their meager existence to support the theological magnificence of the church edifice. Then ask is the sacrifice worth the investment? Did it provide a tangible or an equitable return for the money invested? Did it provide for "daily bread," good shelter, education and world peace.

It is no wonder churches are proselytizing and begging for money.   Do church members ever ask, "Is tithing the poor, ten percent of their income, a mandate from God?" Is it possible that parishioners have been led to believe that for present day donations, they will receive after-death benefits?

A look at the past history of Christianity's grab for power and converts is not very pleasant, but it does give a perspective of the invested value and destructive power of religious beliefs. If all the monetary value acquired by the churches in proselytizing and jockeying for power was balanced against their charitable activities, it may be like a feather trying to tip the scale against an iron pot filled with gold.

Also, the history of the Christian Religion in the United States is certainly something Christians should not be proud of. The Puritans brought the Christian religion to the eastern shores of this great country 500 years ago. With the sheer force of numbers and advanced technology, the white man killed and devastated the Indians tribes with the firepower of guns, with the debilitating influence of alcohol, clear-cutting their beautiful forests, and cruelly killing their wildlife with rifles and steel traps.

A good example is the plight of the Indians in the Lummi Nation. They have 4,026 members remaining and over 1800 are diseased or drug addicted. In order for the healthy to survive, they may have to banish the unhealthy. This is something the tribe considers only under the most severe circumstances. Banishment has been used four times since the arrival of the white man and almost never in a thousand years before his arrival.

Although this devastation was not entirely the fault of the Christians, Christianity was the prominent religion of the early settlers and should have been a stronger influence for love instead of turning a blind eye to American greed and the destruction of a beautiful race of people. The white man came to this new world to escape from the persecution by the European ruling class, only to inflict persecution and killing on a primitive race of people. The white man while living freely, but with little appreciation of their beautiful lands, confined Indians to very small areas called reservations which are the same as small prisons without walls.

Where is the Christian outrage? Where is their love of Jesus to help the Indians? Where were the Indian representatives in the early formed democratic government? Did the Christian religion of love protest the signs "No Indians or Dogs allowed"? Such signs were posted in most white business establishments during the 18th and part of the 19th centuries.

Prior to the landing of the Puritans, the American Indians lived on the lands of the United States for thousands of years in harmony with nature, their God, the Great Spirit, and the environment. In the short time of 200 years, the white man was well on his way of destroying their beautiful forests, killing their wildlife, killing Indian tribes, and grabbing their lands without compensation or payment of any kind. Then to add insult to injury, the Christian missionaries attempted to convert the Indians to Jesus, "A Religion of Love"

How much difference is there when comparing the United States' Indian problem to the plight of the Palestinian people following the end of World War II? The Christian World moved thousands of Jewish settlers into the Middle East, and this invasion of Jewish settlers once again created the great dissention between the Jews and the Palestinians. The educated adults of the Palestinians and the educated adult Jews have never been able to create a peaceful solution for these two races to live within the same proximity of each other without violence and killing. Yet their children who have been educated together, have played together, competed together, and developed friendships together until their adulthood. Then, they took up the fight of their elders!

Now the short sighted Christian wonders why there can't be peace in the Middle East. The solution is simple. First, you prevent all adults from coming to the peace table. Next, give children the education of love and have them sign the peace accord. Then have the United Nations oversee that adults carry it out. It is written somewhere in the Bible, "Let the little child lead them." Why is it so difficult to negotiate and govern with love instead of hate? If both sides could set aside their divisive theology and religious polarization and express love instead of hate in all their negotiations, there would be no Middle East Problem! Jeff Greenfield, a prominent news analyst, said on national TV, "Why can't the peoples of the world work together as friends instead of enemies?"

Doesn't it seem strange that a country which is predominately Christian and is led by Christians, seems to be the most troubled with drug addiction, hated by non-Christians, blatantly corrupt in its corporate power and also with some of its political policies? Could this be another indication that somewhere there is an aberration of the real, true Christian doctrine? This aberration seems particularly obvious with our preemptive involvement in a very hateful, controversial war.

There is no doubt that within the Christian doctrine there is a great store of untapped knowledge about healing that could promote love and world peace, but apparently, time-worn theology has buried it. It seems that the old adage still applies: "By their fruits, ye shall know them."

THE INQUISITION

The following excerpts of information were taken from the New Columbia Encyclopedia; Columbia University Press.

The Inquisitional Tribunal of the Roman Catholic Church was established in the middle Ages for the suppression of heresy. In the early Middle Ages the investigation of heresy was the duty of the bishops.

In 1233, Pope Gregory IX formally established the papal Inquisition, dispatching friars to the south of France to conduct inquests. When the inquisitor arrived in a district, a month of grace was allowed to all who wished to confess and recant; these were given a light penance which was to confirm their faith. After a period of grace, persons who had not abjured were brought up for trial. The defendants were not given the names of their accusers, but they could name their enemies and thus nullify any testimony from these persons. After 1254, the accused had no right to counsel, but the accused found guilty could appeal to the pope. The trials were conducted secretly in the presence of a representative of the bishop and a stipulated number of laymen. Torture of the accused soon became customary and notorious despite the long standing papal condemnation of torture. Pope Innocent IV ultimately permitted torture in cases of heresy. Most trials resulted in a verdict of guilty.

The verdict and the sentence by the inquisitor were enforced by the local ruler. Only heresy was considered a civil and a spiritual offence. Burning at the stake was thought to be fitting punishment for unrecanted heresy. This was probably analogous with the Roman law on treason. However, burning of heretics in the Middle Ages was not common. The usual punishments were penance, fine, and imprisonment. A verdict of guilty also meant confiscation of property by the civil ruler who might turn over part of it to the church. This practice led to graft, blackmail, and simony. It also created suspicion of some of the inquests. Generally, the inquisitors were eager to receive abjurations of heresy and avoid trials. Their purpose was to win back the heretics rather than burn them. The institution which became known as the Roman Inquisition was intended to combat Protestantism, but it is perhaps best known historically for its condemnation of Galileo.

THE SPANISH INQUISITION

The Spanish Inquisition was independent of the medieval inquisition. It was established by King Ferdinand and Isabella with reluctant approval of Pope Sixus IV. It was entirely controlled by Spanish Kings. The Pope's only hold was naming the Inquisitor General. The Popes were never reconciled to the Spanish institution which they regarded as usurping the church's prerogative.

The purpose of the Spanish Inquisition was to discover and punish Jews and later Muslims who were insincere. However, soon no Spaniard could feel safe from it. The Spanish Inquisition was much harsher, more highly organized and far freer with the death penalty.

The Spanish Government tried to establish the Inquisition in all of its dominions, but the Spanish Netherlands and local officials did not cooperate, and the Inquisitors were chased out of Naples in 1510 with the Popes connivance. The Spanish Inquisition was finally abolished in 1834.

Present-day leaders of the Catholic Church have apologized for the actions of the church leaders during the Inquisition period.

WITCHCRAFT

In effort not to lose the perspective of a church-dominated government and loss of freedom, the following pages present a brief history of witchcraft and the church-led Inquisition

Witchcraft is defined as the exercise of supernatural powers mainly for evil purposes through the use of sorcery, black magic, enchantment, Sadism, and other cult arts. The origin of the witchcraft in Europe is found in the pre-Christian, pagan cults such as the Teutonic nature cults in the Roman religions and the speculations of the Gnostics, the Zoroastrians and the Manicheans.

The Pagan religions and philosophies believed in a power of evil and the power of good within the universe. Later among certain sects, their worship of good was repudiated as false and misleading. The Canines, a Gnostic sect, maintained that all that was commended by the Bible as good was in fact evil, and conversely, all that was condemned as evil, was actually good. And finally, they professed that Cain and his rebels were to be admired, and Judas Iscariot was considered the only true apostle.

As the influence of the Christian church spread in the western world, it banned pagan beliefs and practices. Although many of the common people and clergy retained faith in the old beliefs, the church seeking to convert all the peoples of Europe to Christianity was particularly hostile to witchcraft. This attitude however, resulted in the spread of witch lore in an explosion of fear and mass hysteria.

The religious persecutions of supposed witches commenced early in the 14th century. Trials, convictions, and executions became common throughout Europe and reached its peak during 16th and 17th centuries.

Under the authority of the Spanish Inquisition, as many as 100 persons were burned at the stake in a single day. The auto-da-fe, as this mass burning was called, took on the qualities of a carnival, where one could buy souvenirs, rosaries, holy images and food.

Superstition fell on many who were interested in scientific experimentation. An accusation of witchcraft became a means of destroying an enemy or confiscation of an estate. This crusade lasted from the 14th to the 18th century. The colonies of North America shared in this fantasy, particularly, in Salem Massachusetts. Witchcraft still exists in technologically developed societies as well as in contemporary primitive cultures. According to its believers, sickness, disease, misfortunes, and death are caused by witchcraft.

Witchcraft is an example of the harm that results from believing in a lie. But how is it verified that witchcraft is an imaginary fabrication and not a powerful reality? The power of the lie is proportional to the power behind its belief. The devotees of witchcraft found justification for their beliefs in the Holy Bible. How does one decipher truth from fiction if contrasting ideas are presented as the truth in the Holy Bible, and every word in the Bible is considered the word of Truth?

Fortunately, man is endowed with intelligent reasoning and common sense. The use of these two faculties has enabled man to overcome great odds for his well being and survival. In this present age of technology, knowledge is rapidly increasing, and let's hope that with these two faculties, it will increase to greater use in the future.

PRESENT DAY PROBLEMS FACING THE
CATHOLIC CHURCH

Excerpts taken from a front page article in the New York Times delineate the problems

TRAIL OF PAIN IN CHURCH CRISIS
LEADS TO NEARLY EVERY DIOCESE
THE NEW YORK TIMES
Sunday, January 12, 2003
By Laurie Goodstein

The sexual abuse crisis that has engulfed the Roman Catholic Church in the last 12 months has now spread to nearly every American diocese and involves more than 1,200 priests.

These priests are known to have abused more than 4,000 minors over six decades. The New York Times survey, the most complete compilation of data on the problem available, contains the names and histories of 1,205 priests. It counted 4,268 people who have claimed publicly, or in lawsuits, to have been abused by priests. "This has been going on for decades, probably for centuries." said Richard K. O'Connor, a former Dominican priest, who says he was one of 10 boys sexually assaulted by three priests in the South Bronx parish in 1940.

The extent of sexual activity between priests and nuns is not known but it is assumed there are many cases where nuns have had abortions to cover up transgressions, or from being raped by priests. The sex drive among human beings is one of the strongest inherent in man and it is considered to be normal that there should be sex between a man and woman, or that it may occur between a priest and a nun.

It is surprising that Pope John didn't recognize this problem and allow church leaders to marry. They join the lay church members in marriage under the auspices of their God. Why couldn't they join church leaders under that same God? Can the church hierarchy prove that their God requires celibacy for church leaders?

It is estimated that this church has millions of members. This must be an indication of the love the church leaders express to draw such numbers of members. Why doesn't the church use this love to solve its problems instead of paying money to cover-up illegal activities?

The pattern of sexual abuse and cover-up by the church hierarchy could indicate that preserving church prestige is more important than preserving the moral values or adhering to the civil laws within the residing country.

How can any church doctrine withstand the removal of morality and honesty and still remain a viable doctrine?

There is a crisis arising in the Catholic Church starting in the United States. Will it spread worldwide? Recently the Pope acknowledged there are abuse cases in Europe.

In an Era of Change, a persistent Crisis:

June 12 - 15, 2002, US Bishops meet in Dallas to hear testimony from abuse victims and agreed on a new policy to oust all priests suspected of abusing minors.

Oct 18, 2002, The Vatican substantially revises the Dallas policy saying accused priests must be judged by a tribunal made up of priests.

Dec 13, 2002, Cardinal Bernard Law resigns after the judge unseals more documents revealing he knowingly reassigned priests who had sexual relations with girls, boys, and women.

NEW YORK TIMES
THE EDITORIAL BOARD

Boston, March 29 (AP) Bishop Richard G. Lennon, interim leadership the Archdiocese of Boston, has met for the first time with a group representing people abused by clergy members and heard their concerns about how the archdiocese has handled the problem.

The group members said that, "They had asked Bishop Lennon to tell the archdiocese's lawyers to stop what they called hardball tactics."

END OF A PARTIAL EXCERPT FROM THE NEW YORK TIMES
Comment

The preceding pattern of sexual abuse and cover-up by the Catholic hierarchy may indicate that preserving church prestige is more important than preserving moral values or adhering to the civil laws within the residing country.

1. With a billion Christian converts in the world, is this an indication that by sheer numbers alone, people can feel the comfort of a religion that blatantly uses superstition and mythology to hold converts in religious bias? Does this show that belonging to a

religion is more important to converts than questioning its logic or understanding what its doctrine entails?

Does the shooting off of firecrackers on the steps of the church really scare away the evil spirits so that uneducated peasants can come in and pray? Are pictures of Christian Saints bleeding blood at certain times of the year believable? Is the process of exorcism to rid a convert of demons an act of God? Do members of the Christian Churches who give sainthood to another mortal really believe that they are acting out God's will? Aren't these examples of the blind acceptance by converts of a religious doctrine that even the Muslims might find questionable? Unless of course, the church can prove that all these acts have a basis in truth.

WOMAN

Women comprise fifty per cent of the human race. And under a just God they are entitled to fifty per cent of the amenities enjoyed by men such as education, personal freedoms, etc. A woman's devotion to a man is the greatest asset a man can have. Shouldn't a woman be protected from harm? Shouldn't she be loved and cherished and treated as an equal? Shouldn't she receive all the consideration under the law as her male counterpart? Unfortunately, religious concepts are responsible for some of the worst abuse and unfair treatment of the fair sex the world over.

Under the doctrine of Muslim religion, women are raped without recourse. They are flogged if they attempt to escape from under their uncomfortable attire of concealing robes. They are treated as objects of purchase for sex with very little respect or protection under the Muslim law.

The following are excerpts taken from a story of the religious conflict between the Christian and Islamic people that appeared in the Seattle Times.

"A War Only God Sees" March 26, 2001. It is another example of the mutilation of women under Muslim Law.

Amboon, Indonesia--her home destroyed and her church burned to the ground, 14-year old Marina Rumsakur knew there was only one way to survive; convert to Islam and submit to the painful rite of mutilation.

Trapped by Muslim extremists on the tiny island of Kesui, she and more than 900 fellow Christians surrendered. Hundreds of Catholics and Protestants were forced to undergo female excisions or male circumcision with kitchen knives or razor blades as the island was purified of all its Christians. The victims ranged from a 6 year old girl to a 74-year-old woman. "If we did not convert, they would cut our throats," the teenager recounted.

The people of Kesui have been caught up in a vicious war of religious cleansing that has swept through Idonesia's Maluku Islands over the past two years. Largely hidden from the outside world, the conflict has claimed at least 5,000 lives, and has driven 500,000 people--a quarter of Malukus population--from their homes.

THE ABUSE OF NUNS

Another article, "The Abuse of Nuns," reported by Chris Hedges, appeared in the New York Times, March 25, 2001, as follows: "Five confidential church reports by senior members of women's religious orders and an American priest were alleged to have had widespread sexual abuse of nuns by priests in developing countries. Most examples cited in reports, written over the last seven years, occurred in Africa, where about 12 per cent of the world's billion Catholics live. Some involve priests who forced nuns they impregnated to have abortions. The reports say the church has not punished guilty priests. The Vatican responded that there were instances of abuse, but most were confined to a small area.

SAUDI ARABIA

To date, in the month of April, Year 2001, Riyadh, Saudi Arabia, Saudi Interior Minister, Prince Nayef, reaffirmed that his government has no intention of allowing women to drive cars. Women, who wish to draw money from the Bank, must use family ID cards that identify them as dependents of their father or husband. They cannot travel, pursue higher education, nor get a job without written approval of a male guardian. Women's rights are a world wide problem, but in the Middle East they are an extreme problem!

In the United States, some members of the Christian Right are taught that women are inferior to men. Also, U. S. women had to endure a long, difficult battle to get the right to vote. Today, with our advanced technological thinking, women are still fighting for equal pay for equal work, for the right to have control over their own bodies and to have the same sexual freedom enjoyed by men. They are in a difficult battle over abortion rights with the Christian Right's third world thinking and archaic beliefs. At the present, many third world societies are ruled with sixth century, religious mores. Women are still being stoned for adultery. It still takes two for a sexual intercourse; yet, what man in history was ever stoned for adultery?

If the Christian Bible was written with God's guidance as promulgated by the Christian ministry, surely these injustices should have been recognized by a just God who would have given definite instruction to correct injustices. There is no mistreatment of the female species by the males in wildlife; why should there be mistreatment of the human female by their God-fearing males? Is it possible that according to the beliefs of the Christian ministry and the Muslim clergy, as they interpret their Bibles, that God does not have the same love and consideration for the human female as He has had for the wildlife female? Is there any reasonable religious thought that can logically justify the mistreatment of the human female?

Because a women's body is smaller and weaker than the male body, she has been dominated and bullied by men. The assumption has been that the great creator created man stronger than woman; therefore, he must also be wiser. That line of thinking is apparent in biblical literature that portrays the thinking of the nomadic tribes where survival depended on the physical strength of their male partners. Unfortunately, the thinking of the Christian Right, along with the Muslim Clergy, still holds tenaciously to the sixth century concept of the inferiority of women to men.

In our modern, civilized, free society where physical strength no longer plays a role for survival, women are now proving their talents and wisdom by taking their proper place as mental equals to their male counterparts.

What man on earth can prove that God has less love and respect for the female of the species? Among many of God's creatures in the wild, the female is the superior of the species. Isn't it possible that it may be true in the human race also, but man may be too egotistical to recognize or admit it?

William B. Fotheringham

SAUDI'S HOLY WAR WITH AMERICA

(Article in the Seattle Times Sept. 12, 2001
By Kathy Gannon; The Associated Press

In the Middle East the problems are with the men, not the women. Osama bin Laden is considered the architect of some of the worst acts of violence and terrorism in the United States (US).

Kabul, Afghanistan--highly coordinated and unprecedented in scale, yesterday's attack in the United States put the spotlight on the man suspected of orchestrating some of the world's worst terrorist acts--Osama bin Laden.

The United States has called bin Laden the architect of terror after the 1993 attack on the World Trade Center, the 1998 bombing of two U.S. embassies in Africa and last year's bombing of the USS Cole in Yemen.

The FBI has a five-million-dollar bounty on bin Laden's head. The State Department calls him the most significant sponsor of Islamic extremism in the world today.

Stripped of his Saudi citizenship, bin Laden is thought to have been hiding for the past five years in Afghanistan under Taliban protection. He has repeatedly called on Muslims worldwide to join in the jihad, a holy war, declared on the United States in religious edicts faxed to the outside world. All US citizens are legitimate targets.

The Al-Qud Fal-Arabia newspaper quoted bin Laden as saying, "I am fighting so I can die a martyr and go to Heaven and meet God." "Our fight now is against the Americans." In May, bin Laden instructed activists attending a Muslim convention in Afghanistan to prepare the next generation for jihad. "Issue a call to the young generation to get ready for the holy war and prepare for that in Afghanistan because the jihad in this time of crisis for Muslims is an obligation for Muslims.

END OF EXCERPT
Comment

Among the millions of average Muslims, bin Laden is an extremist. The Muslim God is attributed to have the following concept: The Muslim God loves the ink of scholars more than the blood of martyrs.

Whether bin Laden is responsible for destroying the one hundred ten stories of the World Trade Center's twin towers which killed 3,500 people, it is too soon to determine, but the experts on terrorism view the prospect of his guilt is reasonable as leader of al Qaeda

As a result of this attack a major segment of the United States Financial Center was destroyed adversely affecting the economies and stock markets world wide. The U.S. declared war on the terrorists and on any country that harbors them. This is, yet, another example of the religious extremists' mythological beliefs, with no proof of truth that could possibly propel two countries into war.

What is most obvious in this terrible conflict is the view that the God of bin Laden will condone this attack on an American city. All of bin Laden's acts of terror are predicated on the unsubstantiated belief that he may die a martyr and live peacefully beside Allah in the Muslim Heaven. Is it logical that Allah's earthly followers will kill Christians while Allah lives peacefully in the Muslim Heaven? Is the Christian God, Jesus, above this conflict? Is He living peacefully in the Christian Heaven while Christians kill Muslims. Are all these actions logical? Do Muslims and Christians have two different Gods and two different Heavens, but share the same Devil, Hell and fight each other in a Holy war?

Osama is an individual with the potential to destroy a large part of Mother Earth without the slightest consideration that his religious concept could be an aberration of the truth. In his dementia, his interpretation of the Koran is all the authority he needs to commit acts of terror. This view of bin Laden is supported by an article in the Seattle Times, Sept. 12, 2001; by Kathy Gannon of the Associated Press. "Saudi's Holy War With America."

As it is recorded, Jesus never committed acts of violence, but in his name, some of his followers do. Whether or not Allah condones terrorism, his extremists believe he does. All acts by extreme zealots are the result of their mental sickness. It should be the responsibility of the religious leaders to recognize zealots, and give them proper guidance away from violence. This would do more for world peace than any sermon they could preach.

Throughout the Middle East countries where the Muslim religion is the law of the land, women have second class citizenship. The following article displays another example in the country of Iran where religious beliefs thwart justice, individual freedom, and condone murder.

(excerpts are taken from the following article:)
SLAYING MAY HAVE POLITICAL TIES
Seattle Times; Section A; Page 12
By Michael Slackman
Los Angeles Times, July 7, 2001

A holy city in Iran --- Draped head to toe in black chador designed to protect female modesty, the women stood quietly by the road. When a white sedan pulled over, the woman jumped in without hesitation. She said her name was Simin Hossinsi and her price was $5.

Maybe she was tired, desperate, or most likely both. But she insisted that she wasn't worried about getting in the car with a stranger even though a serial killer has been targeting women who sell themselves on the streets of Iran's holist cities.

Prostitution and slaying would be horrible partners in any country. But throw in religion with politics and a chilling murder mystery becomes an exploration of core challenges facing the Islamic Republic from its battle with secular ills to larger questions about the nature of its system of government.

The killings have become another front in the battle between conservatives and reformers seeking to loosen the controls of the ruling leadership. Some think the killings are a cold-blooded conspiracy aimed at undermining moderate President Mohammad Khatami who tried to open the society and force it to confront difficult social issues.

If the women's slayings are a plot to bolster the hard-liners cause, it has seriously misfired. The killings have compelled the leadership to acknowledge that its faith-based society is susceptible to the same kinds of problems as secular societies.

Local newspapers suggested that the killings were the work of religious vigilantes. The news was read with interest in Mashhad, but with great concern in the capitol of Tehran. The reformed-minded parliament ordered an inquiry and summoned the Intelligence Minister for questioning. Investigative members of the parliament said they weren't satisfied with the answer that they had received, on April 1, with the death toll standing at nine the investigative team was replaced with a special squad from Tehran. The investigation has been slow-moving and while reformist lawmaker, Tajermia, blames conservative forces for trying to thwart the probe, local customs and values have also played a part.

The women's families, for example, are so ashamed by the circumstances of the deaths that no one has come forward to claim a body, let alone press for justice. There is no pressure from the community to make an arrest. One civic leader, who runs the social outreach program, pointed out that strict Islamic law, known as Sharia, calls for prostitutes to be stoned-- which generally leads to death.

The following is a synopsis of the plight of second class women under a religious mandate in the Far East.

SOCIALLY OUTCAST INDIAN WIDOWS
EKE OUT LIVING CHANTING HYMS
The Seattle Times News, Wednesday , April 3,2003
By
Sugita Katyal

Reuters

Vrindavan, India Bokul Mara was married at five and widowed just five days after the wedding.

Today, the 75 year old lives alone and abandoned in a dingy room in the north Indian town of Vindavan, chanting Hindu hymns in a temple to earn five rubies(10 cents) a day and an occasional handful of uncooked rice.

"I was of no use to anybody because I couldn't get married again my caste doesn't allow it." whispered Mara as she sat curled on the steps of the temple where priests and pilgrims jostle for space with cows and rickshaws . "So I came here to be a servant of the Lord Krishua," she sighed as she pulled her dirty white sari over her head. Shaven by the monks to mark her widowhood.

Mara is one of 15,000 desperately poor Hindu widows who spend their lives as dais, servants of God, in the dusty town of Vrindavan because they have nowhere else to go.

Shunned by their families and social outcasts because they are considered unlucky, the women come to Vrindavan because they believe they can achieve moksha, or freedom and rebirth from the cycle of birth and rebirth if they devote their life to prayer in the Hindu god Krishuna's hometown.

IN INDIA, A WOMAN IS REVERED ONLY AS A MOTHER, DAUGHTER AND A WIFE

MOHINI GIRI

New Delhi-based women's activists

END OF PARTIAL EXCERPT FROM THE SEATTLE TIMES

Comment

This was another example of the terrible restriction of individual freedom that religious belief can instill on devout believers. Is this practice a stupid waste of women's lives? Or can this be God's plan? What proofs do theists have that this is God's plan? Christians have the same obdurate convictions that "being saved" is God's plan for Christians. Is there any proof that either of these beliefs have validity?

A MUSLIM TRAGEDY

THE PILGRIMAGE TO MECCA

This is another example of a religious ritual in the world because of beliefs in the Devil, and Allah, that was cited in an article in the Seattle Times, Tuesday, March 6, 2001. It described a pilgrimage stampede in Mina, Saudi, Arabia. The annual hajj brought an estimated two million pilgrims to a sprawling tent city in Mina.

There were 35 Muslims trampled and crushed during the Stoning-the-Devil Ritual at the hajj. One witness said, "The stampede started early in the morning and was brought under control three hours later." When older people in the crowd could not move as fast as the others, they were trampled and crushed to death. It was reported that 23 women and 12 men were killed.

Security and safety have been a major concern at the hajj. The annual pilgrimage, according to Islam, must be performed once in a lifetime by every Muslim who is able to do so. Hundreds of hajj pilgrims have been killed in stampedes in recent years.

Pilgrims come to Mina from the holy city of Mecca to cast pebbles the size of chickpeas at three columns of stone that symbolize the Devil as they chant, "In the name of God, God is great."

Once they have completed the stoning ritual, pilgrims shave or clip their hair and then slaughter more than a half million camels, cows, and sheep near Mina, a city that comes to life only during hajj.

The mix of languages and people of different races make crowd control a real challenge for the security forces and the police. The pilgrims usually move in national groups with their leaders carrying flags for identification.

The following are reported past disasters during the hajj, the annual Mecca pilgrimage:

Dec 4, 1979, seventy five Sunni Muslims extremists who had taken over the Grand Mosque in Mecca were killed in a gun battle with the Saudi police.

July 31, 1987, 402 people, mostly Iranian pilgrims, were killed and 649 were wounded in Mecca in a clash with security forces when they staged an anti-U.S. demonstration.

July 9, 1989, two bombs exploded in Mecca killing one pilgrim and wounding six others.

July 2, 1990, 1,426 pilgrims were killed in a stampede in an overcrowded tunnel leading to the holy sites in Mecca.

May 23, 1994, 270 pilgrims were killed in a stampede in Mecca as worshippers surged toward a cavern for the symbolic ritual "Stoning-the-Devil."

April 15, 1997, fires driven by high winds tore through the sprawling, overcrowded tent city trapping and killing more than 340 pilgrims and injuring 1,500.

April 9, 1998, some 180 were trampled to death when panic erupted after several fell off the overpass during the "Stoning-the-Devil" in Mecca."

End of Article

Comment

Is the stoning worth the hundreds of deaths of the pilgrims and the carnage of animals? The Muslim answer is yes. This ritual is sanctified by Mohammed the Arab Prophet, and Allah, in the Muslim Heaven. If Christians joined this ritual and converted to Allah instead of Jesus, they, also, may be assured a place in the Muslim Heaven. Otherwise, they will probably go to Hell—not the Christian Heaven.

Isn't the thought behind this ritual similar to Christian rituals where physical participation is required for mental purification? Christians baptize in water, sip wine, eat bread, roll on the floor, genuflect to a higher power, etc. How, then, can Christians prove to Muslims that the Christian God is the only God? The Christian Bible is not acceptable proof for Muslims. They have proof of their God with their own Bible. If numbers of converts offer validity, the Muslims have their millions with a growing number of converts daily, including world leaders.

Before born-again Christians start their march to the Christian Heaven, maybe they should consider the proof that the Muslims offer for their Heaven with Allah. Both of these belief systems should consider what proofs they are able to give for their theological beliefs other than their Bibles. Is either one of these religions able to prove that their individual God not only exists, but is a viable force for good that ensures present-day benefits, as well as after-death benefits, for all converts?

PROBLEMATIC POL.ITICAL CONSIDERATIONS

Unifying religious beliefs seems to be an impossible task. In the face of world disaster, would political unification also be impossible? The world is not only getting smaller through lines of communication, but the activities of one nation may jeopardize the livelihood of another nation. In past history, confrontations between nations could provoke a basis for war without a threat to the world. With the threat of nuclear annihilation of the world from only one war, there is a need now for a governing body with enough power to mitigate every conflict between nations. As distasteful to every nation's national interest is the concept of subordination to a world body, eventually for world survival, it must be done!

The only entity that comes close to a world governing body is the United Nations (U.N.). It is an organization formed in 1945 by a permanent charter, ratified by 50 countries to pledge for world peace, international laws and treaty obligations that promote security and social purpose. Yet with a pledge to these lofty ideals, presently no nation is willing to subjugate its national interests to this world body. It is becoming very apparent that world interests must come before national interests for world survival; just as individual interests must be subjugated to the laws set by the community.

As an example, suppose the destruction of the world's forests were about to deplete a global source of oxygen. Countries with large forest lands would have to place the control of those lands in a world governing body. Countries that contain rain forests would be expected to give up marketing their rare wood products. These are examples of subjugating national interest to world interests for world survival. Presently, national interests take precedence over world interests. When will national subjugation to the U.N. occur? It may never occur until the destruction of the earth is too far gone for man to stop its bleeding. Then hindsight knowledge will be just another step toward infinite knowledge.

CHAPTER III

DIFFERENT VIEWS OF GOD

A SMALL SAMPLE OF MODERN RELIGIOUS BELIEFS

I. al Qaeda The Muslim Religion

al Qaeda's message to the United States: to be our friend instead of our enemy, the United States must: 1. Drop its support of Israel. 2. Convert to Allah instead of Jesus.

II. The American Indian believes in the Great Spirit

Oh Great Spirit
Whose voice I hear in the winds
Whose breath gives life to the world
Hear me
I am small and weak
I need your strength and wisdom
May I walk in beauty
Make my eyes behold the red and purple sunset
Make my hands respect the things you have made
And my ears sharp to your voice
Make me wise so that I may know
The things you have taught your children
The lessons you have written
In every leaf and rock
Make me strong, not to be superior
To my brothers
But to fight my greatest enemy-
myself
Make me ready to come to you
With straight eyes
So that when life fades as the fading sunset
My spirit may come to you without shame

Chief Yellow Lark, Sioux

American Indian's view of death

> Do not stand at my grave and weep
> I am not there. I do not sleep
>
> I am the thousand winds that blow
> I am the diamond glint on the snow
>
> When you wake in the morning hush
> I am the swift uplifting rush
> Of quiet birds in circling flight
> I am the soft starlight at night
>
> Do not stand at my grave and weep
> I am not there. I do not sleep
> Indian Author Unknown

III. The Baptist Church

Common with most Christian churches, this church accepts Jesus as their personal savior and strives for advancement of this church in knowledge, holiness and comfort, to promote its prosperity and spirituality.

This church teaches that angels are beings higher in order of creation than man, but not to be worshipped by man. Satan is a fallen angel who rebelled against God.

Physical death involves no loss of consciousness. The soul of the redeemed passes immediately into the presence of Christ. There is a separation of soul and body until the first resurrection of Jesus; then soul, spirit, and body will be reunited forever in the Lord Jesus Christ. The personal return of Jesus will reward the redeemed according to their works.

IV. The Catholic Church

They teach that the pope is God's representative here on earth. The Virgin Mary is in Heaven and hears the prayers of the Catholic parishioners here on earth.

They teach that God is the Father, the Son, and the Holy Spirit. They teach that there is a Heaven, Purgatory and Hell. They teach that only those who are trained in the catechism of the church are qualified to interpret the scriptures for the laity of the church.

V. The Christian Church

They are a family of believers who accept each other because God accepted them. They have no creeds. The Bible is their only text book and is the final authority in doctrine. They teach that God is the Father, the Son, and the Holy Spirit. We all possess the attributes of God.

Salvation after death is the free gift of God. The only sufficient payment for the sins of mankind is the death of Christ who acts as their substitute. No one is saved by his own merits or good deeds. It is necessary to respond to God's free gift of salvation by faith, repentance, and baptism by immersion. God then meets them, forgives them for their sins and gives them the gift of the Holy Spirit.

God gives us abilities that we are to use in service to one another and the world. We do not work and serve to be saved, rather to express gratitude for God's gift of eternal life.

VI. The Christian Science Church

Along with all the majority of the religions of the world, they believe in eternal life after death. It is obvious, they insist, that eternal life cannot be dependent on temporal matter for its health or its existence. If God, truth is perfect life, then any imperfection in life (deformity, sin, sickness, disease, or death) is the lie that dissipates before truth. "Ye shall know the truth and the truth will make you free." Jesus. The Christian Science view is that whatever healings were possible in the past have to be possible in the same manner in the present.

Its tenets: 1. As adherents to truth we take the inspired word of the Bible as our sufficient guide for eternal life.

2. We acknowledge and adore one supreme, infinite God. We acknowledge His son, one Christ, the Holy Ghost or divine comforter, and man in his image and likeness.

3. We acknowledge God's forgiveness of sin in the destruction of sin and the spiritual understanding that cast out evil as unreal. But the belief in sin is punished as long as the belief lasts.

4. We acknowledge Jesus atonement as the divine efficacious Love unfolding man's unity with God through Christ, through Truth, life and Love as demonstrated by the Galilean Prophet in healing the sick and overcoming death.

5. We acknowledge that the crucifixion of Jesus and his resurrection served to uplift faith to the understanding of eternal life, even the allness of Soul, Spirit and the nothingness of matter.

6. And we solemnly promise and pray for that Mind to be in us that was in Christ Jesus; to do unto others as we would have them do unto us; to be merciful, just and pure.

VII. The Congregational Church

What is God? God is Spirit. God made everything that was made. The beauty of nature and lives of loving persons were made for our happiness. Everything comes from God. No one has seen God. Being Spirit God is everywhere.

Relationships: We are the children of God. God's laws are righteousness and goodness. No one has kept the laws of God. Therefore, every one is subject to sin. When we are ready to confess our sins in true repentance to God, God will forgive the sinner. It is only through Christ are we saved from our sins. We are meant to live forever. It is only through Christ can one enter Heaven. We accept the Trinity concept of God. We also believe in Heaven, Hell and Satan.

VIII. The Episcopal Church

They believe in the Trinity concept of God. They believe in Heaven, Hell, and Satan. It is only through Christ can one enter Heaven.

IX. Jehovah's Witnesses

They believe in eternal life after death in paradise earth. They believe that God created Adam and Eve in the Garden of Eden and God is Jehovah one God, they do not believe in the Trinity concept of God.

X. The Lutheran Church

They believe in the Trinity. They believe the Apostle's Creed.

XI. The Mormon Church

They do not believe that man's sins were caused by Adam's sin. They believe that each individual causes his or her sins. They believe through the atonement of Christ all mankind may be saved, by obedience to the laws and ordinances of the Gospel. Those ordinances are: faith in Jesus Christ repentance; baptism by immersion for the remission of sins. Lay on hands by those who are in authority to preach the Gospel and administer the ordinances. They believe in the gift of tongues, prophecy, revelation, visions, (that God will reveal many great and important things pertaining to the kingdom of God) and more healings.

They believe all men should worship God according to the dictates of their conscience. They believe in the freedom of religion and being subject to the law of the land.

XII. The Presbyterian Church

We are known as the confessional church. At varying times we have undertaken to confess the state of our beliefs for all the world to see.

Our church is governed by elders. We are a church with a representative form of government by elders elected by the people.

The sovereignty of God is the central sun which everything in our doctrinal system revolves. We cannot over estimate the perfection of God. More significantly, we recognize that our terms of God simply in terms of superlative characteristics can distract us from the essential Reformed Belief that God is known to us primarily in terms of actions rather than in terms of His perfection.

PREDESTINATION

God calls on some human beings to a special relationship and destiny. If one asks why or how God chooses, the only answer we found to be adequate is an affirmation of the sheer mystery of it all. He chooses to choose.

Double predestination is the conviction that if God actively chooses some people, he therefore must choose not to choose some others. The nature of humanity--two basic aspects that need to be held in balance. The first grows from the positive affirmation that God's creation is essentially good. We were made in his image and likeness.

The second word about human nature has to do with the dereliction from the plan that God established. Human depravity is a situation that cannot be reversed. The primary evidence of God's election is a sincere, thorough attitude of repentance. Sanctification is a process of one's growth by God that once begun will not be undone by any power.

We believe that the discipline of the intellect is a very important feature of Christian living. It is very difficult for people to be Christian by themselves because the faith of the individual is dependent on the faith of the community.

XIV.   Radical Islam

On Sunday, April 26, 2003, Seattle Washington, Television Station MSNBC the Mind of the Bomber by John S Thaler was discussed. Bombers whose bombs did not explode were immediately arrested. They were interviewed in prison by the Israeli police. They told how they were recruited and why they became suicide bombers

The radical Islam Hamas are always looking for potential recruits. The criteria for a suicide bomber were (1) their passionate belief in Islam. (2) They were men in their twenties. (3) They felt disenfranchised from society(4) They were very poor and money could be a strong incentive.

If a bomber made a commitment to give his life, he was promised $6,000 for his family which was a very large sum in Iraq.

As soon as a drop of blood is spilled, Jihad will claim victory. The bomber and his family will immediately be forgiven of all their sins and wrong doings. Once the bomber has made a commitment, he must follow through or he will spend the rest of his life in hell. He is told death is a privilege and martyrdom is more important than victory. For each suicide bomber that loses his life, there will be a thousand more to take his place.

After the explosives are strapped on the Muslim bomber, he goes to the graveyard and lies beside his grave stone. There he uses his faith to calm his nerves. He remembers that he is a hero to his family and to Allah. In Heaven he will have 40 virgins to fulfill all his needs and desires.

THE PHILOSOPHER OF ISLAMIC TERROR

By Paul Berman
New York Magazine, March 23, 2003

The roots of al Qaeda are neither in poverty nor in anti –Americanism, but in Sayyid Qutb's ideas about how Christianity went wrong and how martyrdom could change the world. The truly dangerous element in American life wasn't capitalism, its foreign policy, or woman's independence, it was America's separation of church and state.

In the days following September 11, 2001, al Qaeda was driven from its bases in Afghanistan. Arrests and maneuvers occurred daily and are still occurring. Recently one of bin Laden's top lieutenants was arrested in Pakistan. Yet al Qaeda wasn't fazed. Its popularity has turned out to be large and genuine in more than a few countries. al Qaeda upholds a paranoid and an apocalyptic world view that the "Crusaders and the Zionists have been conspiring for centuries to destroy Islam."

Valiant police in many countries have raided a number of Muslim charities and Islamic banks which stand accused of subsidizing the terrorists. These raids have advanced the war on still another front. But the raids have shown that al Qaeda is not only popular but that it is institutionally solid, with a worldwide network of clandestine resources. This is an organization with ties to the ruling elites in many countries.

To anyone who looked closely enough, the al Qaeda organization plainly enjoys another strength that is truly imposing—though in the Western

Press this final strength has received very little attention. Bin Laden is a Saudi plutocrat with Yemeni ancestors and most of the suicide bombers were Saudis. But al Qaeda has deeper roots. The organization was created in the 1980's by an affiliation of three armed factions—bin Laden's circle of Afghan Arabs together with two factions from EGYPT—The Islamic group and the Egyptian Islamic jihad. The Egyptian factions emerged from an older and current school of thought from Egypt's fundamentalists' movement—the Muslim Brotherhood in 1950's and 60's. At the heart of this single school of thought stood until his execution in 1966 Sayyid Qutb, the intellectual hero of every one of the groups that eventually formed al Qaeda. Qutb wrote a book called the "Milestone" which became a classic manifesto of the terrorists' wing of Islam Fundamentalists. Qutb's analysis was soulful and heartfelt. The analysis asked some genuinely perplexing questions about the division between mind and body in western thought as well as about the difficulties of striking a balance between sensual experience and spiritual elevation. He poured his ideas through a filter of Koranic commentary and the filter gave his commentary a grainy new texture, authentic Muslim which allowed him to make a series of points no western thinker was likely to propose.

One of those points had to do with a women's role in society. He understood quite clearly that in a liberal society women are free to consult their own hearts and pursue careers in quest of material wealth. However, from his point of view this could only mean that women had shucked their responsibility to shape the human character through child-bearing. The Western notion of a women's freedom could only mean that God and the natural order of life had been set aside in favor of a belief in other sources and authorities, like one's own heart.

It meant that without a reference to God, the natural order of life had been set aside, and that life had no prospect of being satisfactory or fulfilling. Christianity's ancient division between the sacred and the secular was an ideological difference between Western liberal countries and the world of Islam. Qutb trembled with rage at the effort to push Islam into a corner separate from state.

Their deepest confrontation is not for the control of territories, economic resources or military denomination, it is over Islam. Religion was the issue! This religion of Islam is so intrinsically genuine and so colossally deep rooted that all such efforts to separate it from state control or brutal accusations avail nothing. Islam's true champions are few, but numbers meant nothing to Qutb. The few who gather themselves in what is called a Vanguard to undertake the renovation of Islam and will cause the change of civilizations all over the world.

Qutb wanted a Vanguard vow to live according to Islamic principles and reinstate the Shariah. The Shariah advocated an eye for an eye, cutting off the hands and the feet, stoning for adultery, or flogging from 80 to 100 strokes which usually caused death for those who did not obey the rules of daily life as required by the Koran. Most of all Qutb wanted the Vanguard to accept the obligations of the jihad in the struggle for Islam.

The obligations for the jihad include suicide bombing for the eventual religious rule over secular societies and civil authority. Thus, Islam and the state will become one ruler, and eventually Islam will become ruler of the world

CHRISTIAN FUNDAMENTALISM

If God is Love and Intelligence, then a man who loves and thinks is one with his God. Why do Fundamentalists choose biblical passages that indicate otherwise? Isn't it strange that Fundamentalists use biblical passages that indicate the great schism and alienation between God and man, rather than using biblical passages that express the love and intimacy that exists between God and all his offspring. Both concepts are in the Bible.

The Bible states that, "As a man thinketh so is he." If he believes that he must plead for mercy from a magnified mortal called Jesus, to forgive him for his sins and his existence, he will then have a religion of restriction rather than a religion of assistance.

Fundamentalists use the term "person" to define their concept of God. Billy Graham said in his book that God is like Jesus Christ.

The Webster Dictionary defines person as: a human being, man, woman, or child, a human living body, personality, self, or being.

Typical Christian Ministers view God as Spirit with the attributes and sympathies of a mortal. Is it conceivable for Spirit to sympathize with mortals? Sympathy recognizes misfortunes--the absence of good. If God, Spirit, is recognized as the omnipresence of good, how could God recognize misfortune or sympathize with mortals? Isn't this similar to expecting the principle of harmony in the mathematics of music to sympathize with the musician who could not produce harmonious sound? Or expecting the principle of mathematics to sympathize with the mathematician who kept making mistakes? Errors, misfortunes, weakness, evil with all its forms cannot be recognized as a powerful presence in opposition to the ever-presence of good. By definition there can only be one supreme power that can rule in the lives of mortals. When and how it rules depends on the thinking of mortals.

It is amazing that there are over 100 million Christians who recognize that there are metaphysical laws and principles in chemistry, electricity, mathematics, physics and other sciences that are applied daily for the benefit of mankind. Yet in the field of theology the attributes of God's laws of love, Spiritual-Life power, Purity, and Intelligence are not recognized as laws or principles that can be applied to problem solving for improving human life on earth.

A very brief summary of Billy Graham's book "Peace with God" portrays a view of God that is comprised of a spiritual person with an all-encompassing love for His creation that has been estranged from Him because of Adam's sin. This all-powerful God is helpless to save all of the Christians from evil because of the all-powerful concept of "Free Will" which can lead man to sin and separate him from God. Only if God forgives man for sinning will he be able bridge the schism and get back into God's good graces. The so-called logic of these arguments, according to Billy Graham, can be substantiated by certain passages in the Bible.

For the God-forsaken secular community that cannot accept the concepts of Heaven, Hell. Satan, a talking snake, a fruit tree with evil fruit, Jesus dying on the cross for mankind's sins and other fairy-tale concepts, Fundamentalism offers them no hope for the hereafter. Let us hope that future Christian Ministers and Fundamentalists will expand their concept of Deity beyond the limited concept of a man-God.

SUMMARY OF THE CHRISTIAN DOCTRINE

1. What God is:

God is Love.   God is Spirit, but not the Great Spirit of the American Indians.

A man named Jesus is a God who turned himself into a fetus in Mary's womb. He was born of Mary, the mother of God. Jesus' Father is also God so Jesus is the son of God. There is the accepted concept that the term "Trinity" describes God as Jesus, as the Father and as the Holy Spirit. These three entities merge into one entity called God. In the Christian Bible Jesus is a corporeal man which is different in nature from the Holy Spirit, but He is still God.. The Trinity concept is given special worship on Trinity Sunday in the traditional Western, Christian churches.

2. God's Creation:

God, also the father of Jesus and Adam and Eve, created the world and the universe in six days. He also must have created the Garden of Eden with its tree of evil knowledge. Next He created, in his image, a man, named Adam from the dirt of the Garden. He created a woman, named Eve, from the rib of Adam. Adam and Eve were the first parents of the human race. Then God created all other living beings on the earth. In the midst of the Garden He planted a tree with all the knowledge of evil ingrained in its fruit, and He told Adam not to eat of it. One of the living beings God created was a snake that learned the Hebrew language and then convinced a nude Eve to eat its fruit. This act of eating the fruit angered God; so He sent them out of the Garden and He made the snake crawl on his belly for the rest of his Life. This act of eating also made Adam and Eve realize that it was a disgrace to be seen naked.

And it seems that from an adoption of some part of Greek mythology, Christians believe that somewhere in this universe that God created Heaven, Purgatory, and Hell. (The Greek version of Hell includes Charon, the boatman, who ferries dead souls across the river Styx to Hades). These three places, it is believed, are where all people go after death.. However once there, one will have eternal life. God's help is not available in Hell. There is an ex-angel, named Satan, who rebelled against God, and he is in charge of Hell. It is the Christian belief that He, along with Eve, is the cause of all evil. One can avoid going to Hell by declaring and accepting Jesus as one's personal savior. Through God's gift of a "Free Will." man is able to make choices. God will never interfere with a person's choice. However, a wrong choice could land one in Hell--out of reach of God's help forever.

3. There is a need to support the churches in the United States (US).

The U.S. law precludes the government from giving financial support to churches. The general population must do it! It is very possible that worshipers believe that God will look favorably on people who give money to their church. But there is never enough money; so there is a movement in the US by the Christian Right to change the law that presently prevents any church from ruling over the state or controlling state funds.

THIS IS THE END OF A SMALL SAMPLE OF VARYING RELIGIOUS BELIEFS.

The preceding excerpts, other than the Christian summary, were taken from the literature of each church. The simple beauty and depth of insight of the American Indian's prayer shows a contrast to the small sample of the White Man's religious beliefs. The excerpts, also, give a small sample of the doctrine of al Qaeda. This is only a glimpse into the religious doctrines that comprise a pattern of common ideologies.

How similar are the theologies of the Muslims and the Christians. For example, the parishioners of both religions must make a commitment and honor that commitment in order to go to Heaven. For all Muslims and Christians, death is their only pathway to Heaven. The Christians must make a commitment to Jesus. The Muslims may make a commitment of suicide to Allah. If they break their commitment, they may go to Hell. Both religions have a strong belief in Satan and Hell. Once a commitment is honored, they are exonerated from all their wrong doings and their sins are forgiven. Both religions relate to God's forgiving of sins for a place in Heaven. Many Christian religions and most radical Islams abhor the policy of the separation of church and state.

The message from al Qaeda is an example of the two largest religions in the world about to embark on a war believing their mythical Gods are supportive of their destructive actions. How many centuries ago was it that the Romans and the Greeks believed in mythical Gods as they went to war? Why can't mankind learn from history?

If the leaders of these two religions would promulgate the concept that God is love, would a war be necessary? Wouldn't actions that go against love, be actions that go against their God?

It is interesting to note that there is such an absolute conviction by each ideology that their particular doctrine is incontrovertibly the word of God. In this small sample, most of the ideologies refer: to God as He, Jesus as God, Heaven, Hell and Satan as realities. There is a need for Christians to be saved. Common to many denominations is the belief that Adam's disobedience separated mankind from God, and only through Jesus can one be saved and proceed to the presence of God in Heaven.

Most Christians will acknowledge that omnipresence, omnipotence, infinity, immutability, purity, intelligence, tolerance, love, life, truth and spirituality are attributes that define their concept of God; yet, they accept as true, the thinking and actions of that God that are diametrically opposed to those attributes.

Christians believe that God's omnipresence, omnipotence and goodness do not exist in Hell. They believe that their God, the only creator, is good, pure, and sinless, but that all the humans He created will become sinners. Along with members of the Satanic Cult, they have this concept of Satan as a reality. According to Christian and Muslim doctrine, there is no goodness in Satan. He is thoroughly bad. There needs to be qualities of purity, consistency, common sense and logic in any concept of Deity or that concept will border on the mythological. For example, Christians need to prove that Satan exists and is the source of evil.

A SECULAR VIEW OF RELIGION

Unfortunately in the secular world working out one's salvation is not accomplished on a class action basis through a second party. The diversity of religious beliefs with their vast and insurmountable, multiform ideologies from cult fanaticism to stoics exemplifies the impossibility of standardization and/or the unification of religious doctrines. However, the real, true concepts of God must have a commonality of love and other positive attributes within all religions. Biblical interpretations are thus left to such factors as race (ethnic) and the chance of hereditary influence on the basis of one's particular creed. The sins of one culture could be considered morally acceptable behavior in a diverse culture. Examples are herbal stimulants, alcoholic beverages such as wine and the diet that includes the flesh of cloven hoofed animals considered sacred or sacrificial in one culture and deemed heresy in another culture according to the particular folkways and mores of that society.

Doesn't each group select its own belief in a God or Gods, a supreme being, atheism, or agnosticism? Wouldn't the choice of belief then finally be relegated not by the action of a higher power, but in the definitive decision of each mortal drawing on the limitations of his or her individual capabilities of reasoning, emotional strength, and his or her faculty of logic and education that would make the final determination of acceptance or rejection of a belief or belief system?

Isn't the entire concept of religion similar to the statement "The map is not the territory"? Mankind has created a breathtaking concept and depiction of God or Gods wholly within itself with various interpretations of biblical history passed down through the ages much like the preservation of a language.

Like the children's books of fairy tales and fantasy, the Bible a magnificent book, is a monumental tribute to the desire that there is meaning and purpose for something better and salvation from the mean existence of trials and tribulation in a man's life on earth. This is a challenge each of us must experience until death. And who among us is not without the fantasy for a better life for ourselves, our family, our children and friends. In the entire history of the world, mankind has relied on the fantasy and dreams born from the need to soothe the pain of reality in acknowledging the weakness of mortal flesh. What other solutions to suffering are there than to create a concept of something outside ourselves and mighty enough to solve all our problems and offer surcease. A Supreme Being all seeing, all powerful, and perfect person with a perfect refuge that offers the solution to a pain encountered worldly existence. Could it be that this Supreme being is untouched and impervious to the physical and mental illnesses and the stresses that man encounters in a living world?

The thoughts and actions attributed to this Supreme Being created religions to fill the needs of multitudinous races and cultures. Each religion was fashioned to conform to the immediate society. The mystery of the Supreme Being and his magical healings was in turn embellished as a panacea that was handed down by mouth, by translation and interpretation from father to son over the centuries until the simple hope for a miraculous solution became an enormous commercial and gaudy display of pageantry and ritualism fueled by guilt and retribution of a sin-branded society living a self-fulfilling prophecy.

For religious beliefs to survive the technological age and gain credence in the secular community, the beliefs must be devoid of myths and superstition, must be able to pass the test of simple logic and match the test of truth. Is it possible that a concept of a logical, non-denominational God could unite theologians as well as prove acceptable to the secular field? The many theological beliefs are a very divisive influence world wide, and world leaders must realize that theological problems must be separated from civil authority in order to achieve world peace. It should be obvious that no world leader will rule impartially while openly promulgating a theological concept. Such a rule becomes a breeding ground for insurrection and revolution.

The one undeniable fact that the orthodox Christian churches must eventually face is why there is an absence of Jesus' permanent healing miracles by modern-day Christian Apostles. Are they not the students of Jesus? Isn't Jesus still their Christian teacher? It seems the Christian Orthodox world as students has failed Jesus as their teacher.

Why haven't the Christians looked for the "Healing Miracles" down through the ages to verify and authenticate their religious philosophy? How can an Infinite Spirit in a timeless universe suddenly cease performing the very principles of its existence in healing and providing life without death?

The dichotomy persists that the acts of healing, salvation and resurrection ceased centuries ago despite the assertions that Jesus and God are ever present, eternal entities. Either this healing principle is still in existence today, but modern-day apostles haven't the slightest idea how to find it, or there never was such a principle or a man called Jesus that demonstrated it.

CHAPTER IV
IS A HUMANIZED DEITY A VALID CONCEPT?

HUMANIZED DEITIES: Jesus is God. Allah is God, Buddha is God, Confucius is God, etc. If Christians believe that Jesus is God, how do they prove that their God is not Buddha, or one of the other Gods? Isn't it logical to suggest that the strong belief in Jesus as God unwittingly opens the door to the violence and hatred inherent in anthropomorphic concepts that justify beliefs in other men-Gods? The Catholic and Protestant clergy are oblivious to the great danger they place on this nation by their promulgating anthropomorphic concepts as truth—The United States (US) is the great Satan and Allah hates the followers of Jesus. These are two examples of theological hatred personified!

An example of theological hatred is depicted in a recent film "The Passion of the Christ." This motion picture created and directed by a renowned actor, Mel Gibson, is thought to have become the most popular film to be released in the year 2004. Mr. Gibson, a Roman Catholic, produced his version of the last 12 hours of the Life of Jesus. The picture displayed the savage brutality of the times. It was played so vividly that one woman had a heart attack watching it and later died at a hospital.

The secular community viewed this film as a quality work of art, by both actors and the director, but it is a movie and nothing more than a movie. The actor who played Jesus survived this motion picture. However, the impact this play has had on the religious community is very revealing. Some Christian denominations consider it axiomatic that Jesus' terrible suffering was for the sins of mankind. Some members of the Jewish community fear that the emotional impact this film has had on Christians may ignite a resurgence in anti-Semiticism.

It was reported on ABC's Night Line, a news program, that one Pastor purchased hundreds of tickets to enable his parishioners and converts to see the film. ABC Night Line showed the long lines of movie goers waiting to view the film. Religious leaders believe that this movie will have a positive impact for proselytizing Christianity worldwide. One fact is certain, Mel Gibson and the movie company will make millions of dollars on this film.

The power for one man, portrayed as Jesus, to withstand such brutal savagery, as displayed in this film, reinforces the belief that he must have been a humanized Deity. What is not taken into consideration is that this brutal savagery was the standard treatment for all felons in those times and it was not a special crucifixion for Jesus. However, if the crucifixion was necessary to prove Jesus' doctrine, the film omitted the substantiation of it. Doesn't it seem strange that a display of a savage crucifixion has had such an impact on the Christian world as to reinforce their convictions? Do acts of violence generate solutions without displaying constructive thinking? The reactions to this film by the religious community seem to indicate very vividly that much of religious faith is based on an emotional, subjective level of perception rather than on an intellectual, objective, non-emotional realization that this was the graphic depiction of one man's interpretation of a biblical event.

Many Christians who had an emotional reaction to this film's portrayal of the brutality toward Jesus, must have encountered the question why would a man go through such an ordeal if he had a choice to avoid it? It seems the most obvious answer to that question would be to promote a doctrine that he proved by his "works." At this point of inquiry, are all Christians absolutely satisfied with their church's doctrine that cannot produce healing on demand, yet has promulgated for 2,000 years, a fundamental doctrine that is without proof of its beliefs?

The Christians view the Christian Bible as the absolute word from their Christian God. The Muslims view the Koran, their Bible, as the absolute word from their Muslim God. Is there any room for a compromise? Are these two humanized Gods aware of each other? Is there any common ground between them for developing a peaceful accord instead of a war? Both of these Gods must recognize the attributes of Love, Life, Spirit, Purity, Truth etc. as an integral part of their basic theology. Why do they not practice them? Will all parishioners kill themselves in a war to prove that their God's doctrine is the only truth?

Meanwhile, another religious best seller, "The Da Vinci Code" resulted in a controversial movie. Did Jesus, or didn't he marry a prostitute? Whether Jesus was single, a married man, or gay is not important. What is important is his "works" and the underlying thinking that produced them. Does it matter that the Christian world was stampeded into going in the wrong direction toward anthropomorphism?

Jesus was described as man who healed disease, sickness, deformed bones and overcame death with nothing more than the power of thought. Loving this man as God, while ignoring his doctrine, is a means of worshipping him without doing his works. Rather than learning his doctrine of dominion, man acquiesces to the servitude of sickness, disease and death. He ends his life in a nursing home death-bed. Is this the true role for man as a Christian follower of Jesus?

Somewhere, at sometime shouldn't there be proof that the Gods of the theists do exist beyond the words in their bibles? Doesn't it seem that the first step in developing this proof would be to analyze the concept of anthropomorphism?

GOD AS A PARENT

Most ministers of the Christian faith present a paternal God to their congregations that they talk to as a child talks to a parent. This parent is usually Jesus, the Father, or the Virgin Mary. It is believed that this parent-type God may listen to their petitions and by the will of a parent these prayers may be considered, studied, granted, or rejected. Many Christian ministers tell their congregations that man is not privy to the wisdom of God; therefore, parishioners must accept His will without question, particularly if the petition is not granted. Is it logical that infinite wisdom is contained in a mortal figure that disperses good capriciously to only those of favor?

That is what the term "God's will" implies. When the term "God's will" is accepted as truth by any Christian, it exposes his/her lack of understanding what the term "God" embraces, with all powerful positive attributes.

It is difficult for Christians not to think of God as a father figure when the Lord's Prayer begins with "Our Father which art in Heaven." Jesus also said, "The kingdom of God is within you." How do those two concepts fit together? One statement places God in Heaven far away. The second statement places God inside of oneself, and St. Paul stated that we live and move and have our being in God. The latter concept places mankind inside God--another conflict. The fact that there are conflicting ideas

63

presented throughout the Bible shouldn't prevent a logical premise to be applied to a concept of Deity with or without the Bible.

The fact that the Bible portrays God as a father figure representing love and care for his family doesn't necessarily make God a corporeal being. The majority of Jesus' students were uneducated peasants whose grasp of ideas came more easily in parables and symbolism. What could be a more natural symbol of strength, coupled with care, than the father figure? He was the head of the family, he was the authority, he set the laws that they lived by, and he provided food and shelter. Doesn't it seem logical that their view of a higher power would be symbolized with the authority of a father figure?

As long as Christians retain the fourth century view and logic of God as a man, that view of God will have the idiosyncrasies of a mortal. So the common perception of God will remain as an immortal, mortal who, through Adam, separated himself from his offspring. This view doesn't explain how man can have life without God which is life itself. If a living being expresses life, shouldn't that being also express all the other attributes of God. There can never be a shortage of positive attributes available for use. How can a man express life without love, or love without intelligence or hate without violence? The answer to that question might be that the purpose of living is for man to learn how to separate the good from the bad for a positive life. Isn't that what Jesus portrayed? Isn't the story of Jesus' life, a story of a man exemplifying all of the positive attributes of good? Why do his followers also accentuate the power of evil; thus denying in their lives much of the power of the positive attributes?

The answer might be that man's mind is like a radio station stuck on one station only, closed to all the others. He is not receptive to the power of all the other attributes. They must be available in abundance, but evidently theists have not learned to tune in on them, or else religion would be a massive movement of an all encompassing love rather than a movement of rejection and the selection of the converted few.

When Christians petition their parent--God for their needs and desires, are they not denying the availability of their omnipresent, omnipotent God? If they have a close, loving relationship with their God, why would they have unfulfilled needs? Don't the offspring of good, wealthy parents have their needs and desires met? As an offspring of God, shouldn't man have the talent, intelligence, and ability to fulfill his own needs? It would seem the best sermon Christian ministers could preach to their congregation would be for each member to gain self-knowledge of his God-given talents.

If all the humanized mythologies could be removed from Christianity, none of these parent-type Gods would be part of Christianity. All that would remain of the Christian religion would be the positive, good attributes.

Think for a moment of the statement, "The Kingdom of God is within you." If that is a true statement, then that concept places all of the power of the positive attributes, termed God, as a potential for immediate use by every living human being on earth. Is it possible that this is what Jesus realized and taught his students when they produced all the miracles of healing? His statement indicates that each human being has the potential ability to heal instantly, the most deadly disease and also know the thoughts of others, overcome death, and have the power of God in every thought.

There is a statement by Jesus in the Christian Bible—"Greater works will ye do." If the Christian world would consider that statement as true, doesn't it place some obligation on good Christians to make an attempt to replicate the "works"? Isn't this immediate power of God recognized when men acknowledge the ever-presence of supreme knowledge? Or do theists believe that all knowledge is selectively distributed by the will of God? Some religions believe that sometime in the future God will endow man with the Holy Spirit. Wouldn't this thought deny the omnipresence of supreme knowledge and goodness called God within each individual?

If a man knew how to use this spiritual knowledge, would he need a parent to depend on? If parents instilled this type of knowledge in their offspring, would their offspring need the parents' guidance during the terrible teens and the bumpy roads in life? Isn't this thought, at least, worth consideration?

Wildlife provides a good example of the parent knowing the exact time to turn away from feeding their young and make them learn to feed themselves. Otherwise, the offspring would die waiting to be fed. They set a good example for the human race. Doesn't man need to be the master of his own destiny and not be a weak, petitioning sinner waiting for his parent God to save him from his own weaknesses? If success breeds success, failure breeds extinction. Will Christians ever turn away from petitioning Jesus for their wants and needs and instead, work out their own salvation "with fear and trembling" as stated in their Bible?

William B. Fotheringham

GOD AND MOTHER NATURE

One Entity or Two?

"The sun shines on the just and the unjust." It shines on the little cub bear that wandered away from his mother. The sun is shining on the little cub and his mother. Is the sun responsible for showing either bear where the other bear is? The sun has only one purpose--that is to shine its light. The light enables the bears to see each other.

Are not the attributes of a spiritual God in abundance in the universe? Shouldn't it be the purpose of life for mankind to learn, to see and to use these attributes? Life has no affinity with death. The flora and fauna furnish the earth with their uniqueness of life. From the small insect to the elephant, each species demonstrates an innate intelligence and love as a means of caring for their offspring. Couldn't this demonstration of love and intelligence expressed in all wildlife be an expression of the same Deity that man also attempts to worship and hunters attempt to kill?

If a comparison were to be made between wildlife and mankind in the success of raising their young, all of wildlife would prove far superior to mankind in the categories of parenting, loving, and training their young for survival.

In the United States there are wars between teenage gangs, school dropouts live on the streets assaulting and stealing to live, young girls and boys are trading their bodies for food and shelter. Where were their parents when these teenagers needed to be taught the value of self-worth, education, self-discipline and morality? Our prisons are living proof of man's failure in proper parenting. Violence, murder, and racial hatred, are examples of man's ignorance of the laws of love that are so apparent in Mother Nature where different species live in peace and harmony with each other. Wildlife parenting has been an example of the successful repetition of parenting generation after generation. Only man with his desire to plunder and kill has interfered with wildlife parenting and their habitats to a point where wildlife is being driven into extinction.

Is the life that is expressed in all things that live, also responsible for the death of all things that die? Does Life terminate life? Is the love expressed by all living beings also responsible for hate? No, Mother Nature and

Deity are not a combination of opposites. The violence expressed in Mother Nature, one may argue, exemplifies a God that is a combination of opposites. Every creature of nature is subject to a possible death by hunters, by the food chain, by violent storms, by terrible fires, floods and droughts. As terrible as these destructive elements seem, they cannot be part of the positive nature of life and love. There can be no death in the principle of life, no evil in the principle of good.

In the "Sorry Scheme of Things" it would seem that as man develops a higher sense of intelligence and love, he will eliminate the violent destruction in his life. He could, then, help animals eliminate the violence in the food chain, eliminate the elements that are destroying wildlife habitats, and he could improve the world environment for all living creatures. The animal rights movements seem to indicate a growing proclivity of mankind to preserve and love Mother Nature which is an expression of Love (God).

The love the hunter expresses in his daily family life takes no part, nor is responsible for his sadistic killing of wild animals. If God is love, that love must reign as love. Only by using a higher level of intelligence will the hunter and industry be able to make a better connection with love and wisdom. They could then cease their reckless annihilation of our beautiful planet with its wildlife. Isn't Mother Nature, as with God, pouring forth more beauty, life, love and goodness than man knows how to use or fully appreciate?

It is obvious that there is a lack, worldwide, of man's appreciation of animal life both wild and domestic. In the United States there is common knowledge of the physical torture inflicted by large corporate farms on domestic animals that are raised for the meat market. Young beef steers are kept in large crates until they are slaughtered. Never in their lifetime are they able to lie in the sun or spend time in a pasture. Chickens spend their lifetime in stacked crates or overcrowded feeding troughs until slaughtered. In the South Pacific dogs are also stacked in crates. And one by one they are hung alive by their necks while a butcher killer uses a blow torch to remove their hairy skin. The longer the dog can withstand the torture before dying, the tastier is its meat. Yet, there is no public outrage! Evidently, the love for meat outweighs the love for animals! Or is the importance of expressing Love, not as important as acquiring tasty meat?

All wildlife, worldwide, is facing extinction in their shrinking habitats. They face tremendous cruelty from uncaring hunters. Sportsmen's magazines advertise the latest and most efficient methods of killing wildlife. African elephants are many times wounded fatally and left to die an agonizing death by hunters who know they can return later for their tusks. Mother bears are randomly killed protecting their young. And add to this, the horrible death animals incur with trappers after their skins.

An example of shrinking habitats is the affect global warming is having on the artic polar bears. There was an article in the Seattle Times, June 13, 2006, By Dan Joling; Associated Press of "Hungry bears preying on each other." Longer seasons without ice, keep them from getting to their natural food. U.S. and Canadians scientists, the principal author is Steven Amstrup of the US Geological Survey found the first ever killing of a mother bear in a den after she gave birth to her cubs. Polar bears feed primarily on ringed seals and use sea ice for feeding, mating and giving birth. This shrinking ice may see the disappearance of polar bears before the end of the century.

It was recently reported on TV news that some of the Buffett billions and the Gates billions were to vaccinate millions of third world children. It seems that the Gate Foundation is oriented to saving humans in an over-populated human world. Do either of these men have any thoughts to use some of their billions to preserve the environment? Otherwise, these millions may have the same plight as wildlife--no habitat to support them.

A DIFFERENT STRIPE OF CRIME

Seattle Times; December 8, 2002; By Sharon Cohen; the Associated Press

Alsph, Ill. The trailer loaded with nine tigers and two lions rolled past the wire fenced gates under the cover of darkness so no outsiders were around to see what was about to happen. The heavy double doors lifted and the zebra striped truck that had hauled the trailer from Wisconsin entered the brightly lit warehouse where two men waited inside with hand guns. The driver got out and poked a stick through the slats to prod the trapped animals into position to make it easier for the shooters to take aim.

The gunmen opened fire killing eight tigers. Their work had just begun. All three men dragged the bloodied carcasses out of the trailer. The shooters began skinning the tigers, and loaded them for their final destination: an exotic butcher shop in another suburb of Chicago. The carcasses were hung on hooks, weighed and sold by the pound. But tiger meat, authorities say, was labeled as lion--which is legal to sell.

Two days later the driver of the truck was frustrated. He had a tiger and two lions that were rejected because they were too small. "I'm going to shoot 'em," he warned, "and throw the in a hole."

In search for profit: This secret slaughter in March, 1998, described in court records by two of those involved, was part of a ruthless black market ring that authorities say killed and sold endangered species--tigers, leopards--for tens of thousands dollars. There is an old saying, "That if you can make a dollar off it, there will be someone trying to kill it and sell it."

There may be more tigers in private hands in the United States than in the wild--and chopped up for their meat and hides, they can be worth more dead than alive.

End of Excerpt

In Matthew Scully's book "Dominion," he reports men of influence run an International Safari Club with 32,000 members which is operated for the promotion of hunting as a sport, "It is my heritage," says General Schwartzkopf. It was reported that former President George Bush is also a club member. Ron Marlenee, a former congressman from Montana, distinguished himself by supporting the slaughter of buffalo.

As a club member, a $10,000 payment will guarantee an elephant and $5,000 will get a polar bear. Mr. Scully stated that this club collects $13.2 million a year in dues which makes this club a strong lobbyist for preferential hunting legislation. He also wrote that the Christian Sportsmen's Fellowship Breakfast is a Safari Club tradition, and their motto is "On Target to Catch Men for Christ."

Recently, it was reported on television that a judge of the Supreme Court and the Vice President of the United States, Dick Cheney, were bird hunting together. As a devout Christian, I wonder if the Vice President ever read the Bible's statement, "Thou shalt not kill?" Certainly, he is not hunting birds for food for his survival; so maybe it could be his hatred of birds, or maybe to satisfy his lust for killing? Is it possible that he may be pro-life for the fetus, but not pro-life for birds? Why isn't Mr. Cheney consistent in his belief in God which is a Life source? If he is pro-life for the fetus, shouldn't he also be pro-life for wildlife? What did that little bird do to Dick Cheney to warrant losing his life in such a violent manner and also possibly wounding his mate or part of the flock that may die an agonizing death later. Do bird hunters really know the number of birds they wound besides the ones they kill? If the Vice President is justified in killing birds, maybe God should reconsider creating birds. Perhaps Mr. Cheney feels that there are enough problems in the world without having unwanted wildlife around.

The book Dominion is an enlightening exposure of animal cruelty by the so-called men of God. Their sincerity as good Christians seems a little far-fetched when they relate killing animals to God, or to the ideology of Christ. Is there any passage in the Christian Bible that tells of Jesus going on a Safari? Their Bible states that God is love, and animals reflect love. Animals do not kill for the sport of it! Isn't this is an example of covering the lust to kill with the cloak of Christ? Is the commandment: "Thou shalt not kill" no longer valid with Christian hunters?

Possibly in the future, wildlife hunters (sportsman?) who are killing wildlife into extinction and leaders of industry who are plundering Mother Nature into a wasteland may become more intelligent and loving and no longer find joy in killing and plundering. Let us hope that the average human being may become more sensitive to the destruction taking place worldwide that is threatening all living beings in our world home.

Commercial fishing nets thirty miles long are clearing the oceans of fish. The Russian are drilling deep in Artic ice to explore prehistoric life forms. Should they drill deep enough, they might release pressure from the inner earth as when one opens a champagne bottle. As far fetched as that may be, the melting ice cap is factual. There is a premise by meteorologists that global warming is slowly melting the ice cap which may destroy the earth. The average citizen who buys an insect fogger or bug zapper destroys the food supply for thousands of birds. Our cities are becoming depleted of wildlife. Lawn fertilizers are polluting city storm sewers, immediate lakes and beaches. Meanwhile, industry is polluting the air. And as the air traveling public looks down on the world's mountain ranges, they see bare

70

land where there used to be snow cap peaks which is indicative of clear cutting and global warming. Sulfuric acid that is used in gold mining destroys fertile lands for miles around, and turns pure, living river waters into 30 years of stinking, poisonous pollution. Beautiful forests are turned into barren lands of fallen timber because of clear cutting. Rain forests are disappearing at an alarming rate due to the lucrative market for rare wood. Worldwide, mankind is destroying the earth and living entities on it with complete disregard for life in the present, or in the future. It is sad that there is no worldwide outrage to stop the plunder of our beautiful earth home.

Where is this parent God the whole world prays to? Why can't He use Love to stop all international dissention, killing and destruction? Why, if He were a good parent, wouldn't He have done a better job of raising his offspring?

Is it possible that God is not a huge, parent God that Christians believe in? But rather, is a term for laws that are based on the powerful principle of good—laws which man needs to learn to use against evil, and not wait for his great, parent God to do for him!

THOUGHTS AND ACTIONS

If a Christian has an accounting problem he can't solve, he goes a step higher to an accountant. If it is a legal problem, he goes to an attorney, if it is a medical problem, he goes to a doctor. If the doctor can't solve it, he goes one step higher to his God as his last resort.

In his primary steps to higher power, he does not kneel and plead forgiveness, he does not deprive his body of food by fasting, he does not declare himself a lowly sinner and beg forgiveness from his accountant, his attorney, or doctor, but his whole demeanor changes when he goes beyond the help of man. He is no longer in charge as the one doing the hiring. He becomes a weak, subservient, genuflecting beggar pleading for mercy. He is no longer the proud son of the Almighty. He is the lowly sinner praying desperately for help from an almighty Father figure.

In turning to a higher power there is a common belief among theists that what a man does to his body has a definite affect on the answers that he is seeking from his Father God. Non-Christians and some devotees flagellate themselves with chains, bow to the east several times a day, or do not drive their cars on certain days of the week. Christians deprive their body of certain foods, fast on certain days, prostrate their bodies, roll on the floor, take part in group chants or rituals, have their body dipped in water, eat a piece of bread, sip a little wine, spend hours counting beads, give money to the church and so on.

Do these actions improve thought? Could thought improve without these actions? There is no doubt that actions are the result of thought, and by viewing actions, they will usually give some indication of the thought processes responsible for the actions. Analyzing the actions of men is one method of determining thought. However, if it is necessary for one's Deity to determine thought by viewing actions, that Deity descends to the level of the human limitations by having eyes that see, ears that hear, and a personal mind that can judge. Is the Christian God so supercilious that He will communicate with only those Christians who are on their knees? Is it impossible for a man to stand on his two feet and pray? Doesn't the Bible suggest that when one prays, he should pray in the closet where it is not possible to be heard or seen by men? Isn't this a place where it wouldn't matter what position the body is in, or what actions it was involved in?

Mathematicians and scientists seeking answers to problems do not use physical gyrations to seek truth. Mathematics and the sciences do not seek thoughts, but rather, men seek thoughts of their peers and stretch the limits of their minds in the search of the unknown. This practice has produced fantastic results for science. Couldn't this also work in the field of theology? Isn't the answer to that in the field of Christian ministry? Are their minds so closed with fourth century theological beliefs that going beyond those beliefs to eliminate mythology, ritual and pageantry might be heresy?

Do the overt actions of Christians indicate to their Deity the state of their introverted thoughts? If so, they have now gone the full circle. Their acts of piety will produce thoughts of forgiveness by their God for their sins. Without these actions, would their God know their thoughts in order to forgive their sins?

To summarize all this rhetoric, the principles of mathematics and the sciences do not have eyes to observe the physical actions of men, or analyze the thoughts of the researchers. Thoughts and actions of scientists are analyzed by men of science to determine the results and the logic of the thought processes used in applying the laws of science.

In order for theology to reach this state of inquiry, the laws of theology would have to be immutable, and consistent. It would be impossible for scientists to deal on a scientific basis with a corporeal, parent--God that is mutable, capricious, acting and reacting on an emotional level of operation, as is attributed to anthropomorphism.

Is it possible that theologians believe that the actions of men, whether sincere or insincere, good or bad, important or insignificant, have an affect on Divine intervention? The answer to this question should reveal whether one's approach to a theological doctrine is on a physical or a metaphysical basis. Is there any proof which approach is correct? The answer is no. Both approaches are in the Bible. The answer comes down to whatever meets ones sense of logic.

ON BEING SAVED

Modern Christianity is more oriented toward saving sinners rather than healing the sick. All "born again" Christians have been saved by ministers of the faith, by Billy Graham, or by many priests. They have all declared Jesus as their personal savior, and in return, Jesus has forgiven their sins and will let them enter Heaven. This belief is justified by specific passages they quote from the Bible. Have good Christians given any thought beyond these lines? Does just having faith in a parent God, and recognizing Jesus as one's personal savior give one final justification for the life that was lived? Is this their final great act of achievement before reaching Heaven? As a future entity in Heaven, is each Christian going to comprehend the thought processes of St. Paul, Mark, Matthew, Luke and others who understood Jesus' thoughts and accomplishments? Is each forgiven Christian going to become equal in the thoughts and accomplishments to this elite group?

If Peter, one of Jesus' personal friends and a student, was not saved from a horrible death, why would present-day students fare any better? Isn't the Bible's concept of, "work out your salvation with fear and trembling, or greater works will ye do," no longer valid? Why does gaining knowledge for survival require effort and learning, but becoming eligible for Heaven requires only faith and belief with no effort in learning as a requirement?

Where do Christians learn to replicate the works of Jesus in order to qualify for a place in Heavenly thinking? The Christian Bible stated that if one has the understanding of mustard seed, he could move mountains. How many mountains have the members of the Christian Right moved? If this is an unfair question to ask of sincere Christians, is it an unfair expectation? These are the words of their leader. If this is a very unfair question to ask or an unrealistic expectation, is it fair or realistic for leaders of the Christian faith to assure their congregations that there are various types of life after death when there is not a shred of proof, other than the Bible, that such knowledge exists?

How can the leaders of the Christian faith assure their congregation that they have been saved? Was there absolute proof supplied? From what have the born-again Christians been saved? Is it Hell? A place where an omnipresent, omnipotent, loving God doesn't exist? Is it from the Devil whose existence cannot be proven? Are they saved from the mistakes they made on earth? Is it a sin to make a mistake? Doesn't the old adage still apply, "that one learns from one's mistakes?" Since mistakes may be incurred in learning, are they nothing more than stepping stones to knowledge? Does being saved eliminate the need for the knowledge of healing all types of problems including sickness, disease or death with only the power of thought? Or are those conditions eliminated only in Heaven? Is it reasonable for Christian leaders to give assurances that their interpretation of the Bible is the absolute truth? To assure another's welfare in Heaven is quite a feat. Shouldn't these leaders prove their words by their works? Why would anyone believe in another's communication with God? Or believe that another mortal's interpretation of the Bible is absolute and irrefutable?

One salient observation is the belief that Christians who recognize Jesus as their savior will be saved. If good Christians die, they will go to Heaven. If they are still on earth, no problem for "born-again" Christians, Jesus will return with his forces and fight the war of Armageddon. This war will kill Satan, save good Christians and all will live happily ever after. End of war!

Armageddon is the seventh myth in this writing. Did this war kill, along with Satan, all non-Christians (75% of the world's population) as well as all non-born again Christians? Is the ideology of Jesus going to suddenly change from love to hate? Is love going to fight a war of hate? Is killing and death, which is the opposite of love and life, going to be the final act of Jesus to save all Christians? Why did Jesus have an adverse encounter with death if he needed it to destroy evil? As stated before, how could the act of death finally free most Christians from evil? Is death going to stand at the pearly gates and banish all forms of evil from entering Heaven? Is death the final friend of all Christians? Is eternal life going to depend on death to preserve life? Doesn't the war of Armageddon as a factual event defy common sense? Where do war and hate fit in the definition of God as Love?

With the Dawn of the 21st century's technology, Christianity with its mythological doctrine is losing its appeal to the younger generation. There is a noticeable shift of Christian theology to third world countries where, evidently, the demands for evidence before conversion, and logical analysis of premises are not so great. (See: "The Changing Face of Christianity," by Kenneth Woodward)

To the extent that one's view of God distorts one's sense of logic, or infringes on another person's right of view such as a mandatory acceptance of doctrine (pro-life), there is a need for a logical analysis of what is true.

If a born-again Christian becomes a national leader, his rights to privacy, his sense of logic, what he believes, and how he intends to lead should be open to public exposure. Particularly, if he believes he has been saved. As a leader, he may feel that it is God's will that he save all his constituents the way he was saved. This may introduce the divisive influence of religion into his leadership. At this point of decision, a little introspection should be in order. Shakespeare's adage should still apply, "And to thy own self be true." That involves placing one's religious convictions to the test of logic and to the test of truth. Analyze the death process, analyze Heaven, Hell as a physical location, question the logic of Satan as an evil source, and man-Jesus as God. If Christians are saved, is there proof that the Father God or Jesus was involved? If there is no definitive answer to just one of these questions regarding Deity, then it is a leader's obligation to lead without religious bias.

Shouldn't a saved Christian have complete dominion over sin, sickness, disease and death? Shouldn't he be able to heal others as Jesus' disciples did? And also prove eternal life by eliminating the ravages and limitations of time? Being saved should mean more, and produce more, than just a joyous expectation of life in Heaven without problems. Above all, remember, "To thy own self, be true." Don't be a follower of mob beliefs without proof!

Christianity is the dominate religion of the free world. It has very powerful, universal concepts. Shouldn't those concepts be subject to the test of truth and be incontrovertibly true, free of mythological conceptions and superstitions? If the early Christian healings were miracles produced by mortals, the prophets and by Jesus and his disciples, wouldn't that immutable thinking process be worthy of an analytical research? Why isn't the search for this thinking-healing process a vital priority for all saved Christians who sincerely want to prove that their religion is the word of God? With this healing knowledge, Christians would have proof of their words. They could also save themselves, and not have to depend on Jesus, their teacher, or their Father God, to do it for them.

CHRISTIAN GROWTH AND A HIGHER POWER

Shouldn't the belief in a higher power be an uplifting state of mind for the believer? There seems to be a proclivity for mankind to believe in the existence of a guiding power beyond the recognition of the physical senses.

This belief in a higher power seems to be innate to all races of people, from the primitive people living in the forests to the highly educated in the ivory towers; they all have their concepts of a Deity, a higher power.

The concept of a corporeal, incorporeal God sitting on a throne high up in the universe seems to be a prevalent Christian concept of a higher power. Petitioning this God for help is a common and futile practice among Christians. It is a futile practice because it depicts the higher power in the form of a corporeal idol beyond human reach. Petitioning this idol for help or mercy is common. It places Christian thinking in a begging mode rather than in a positive acting mode. In the begging mode, the power of good is available only by a decision from an unwilling or willing Father God.

Another concept of a higher power is a composite of the positive attributes of good, love, eternal life, truth, spirit, purity and infinite intelligence. All these amorphous entities are useless until they are first recognized and then utilized. Recognizing a positive, metaphysical attribute of love as a power to dispel hate would set in motion actions which would be far different from actions based on hate. The pure concept of life as a power is contrary to thinking of life as temporal, fragile and subject to material forces and death. The concept of intelligence as an ever present power to solve any problem would break the bonds of ignorance. Exercising the purity of concentrated thought in utilizing all of these attributes would be the recognition of a higher power that is far removed from petitioning the gifts of life from a capricious parent God.

Isn't it surprising that many of those higher power concepts held by the elite thinkers of the world, cannot pass the test of simple logic? One example, is that of a United States senator running for the presidency, the highest leadership office in the world, believes that driving a car on Sunday, is at the very least, disrespectful and against the will of his concept of a higher power. Could driving a car on Sunday interfere with worldwide life, intelligence, or love?

Why can't those entities that are greater than man and the world be accepted as an all encompassing higher power? For example, intelligence is a power that motivates thinking in all living beings; love is a power that binds all living creatures together; life is the power to live; spirit is the power behind life and growth, etc. Why can't entities such as these that are a part of all life be recognized as the significant, working knowledge that can be related to a higher power--termed God? Isn't it obvious that thinking confined to a humanized higher power with its mythological concepts for the inexplicable, stunts growth when one is in search for new ideas?

Many times the potential of an individual is curtailed by lack of true self-knowledge, by too much acquiescence to circumstances and adversities that occur daily. It is difficult to surmise how much human potential has been lost by this "born-again" concept. Progress involves the risk of overcoming the status quo. To the extent that this "born-again" concept gives comfort to the status quo, to that extent, it impedes progress. If the Christian will receive ultimate success after death in Heaven, the need to take on the work involved to reach a higher goal on earth may be deemed unnecessary. This belief could result in compromising the individual's God-given talent to the level of mediocrity.

Individuals who have been faced with over-powering obstacles have been known to turn to a higher power for help. The pure faith in a higher power coupled with the refusal to fail has been a great impetus for success. One of the prime elements in success is the refusal to fail.

The accomplishments of the prophets and Jesus as recorded in the Christian Bible, display a very positive line of thinking. They held tenaciously to their concept of what was true in the face of overwhelming evidence to the contrary. As recorded in the Bible, their refusal to accept death as a fact of being enabled Jesus and the prophets to bring the dead back to life.

Whether or not one believes the Bible, or whether the stories of Jesus are true or false, there is a positive thought process in the Bible that is beyond reproach. One outstanding element in Jesus' approach to problems was his faith in a higher power and his relationship to that higher power coupled with positive thinking. What is gained by believing that a higher power is a man-God who determines success or failure? This type of thinking makes man a helpless recipient instead of one who is in control with positive attributes.

We have examples of men overcoming impossible odds at various times in their lives using the force of positive thinking. There are many positive forces that can be identified as a higher power to produce positive results. And these forces are often used in man's extremity. Three of them are life, love and intelligence.

The power to live has denied death many times. Recently, nine miners were trapped 240 feet (the depth equal to a 20-story building) below ground in a tunnel that was rapidly filling with water; yet, they refused to accept death as inevitable. The strong kept the weak from drowning--a real expression of love. The intelligence and love displayed by the rescuers was a successful example of love and intelligence in operation. Intelligence is always available to solve any problem. Unfortunately, fear and other negative emotions interfere with the needed connection to a higher power.

For every conflict, problem or challenge, the Christian who adheres to Jesus teachings should be in control of them. This is particularly true if he is learning from the lessons taught by his teacher, Jesus. The Bible records Jesus as being in absolute control in every situation. He taught his pupils to do the same. In every case of sin, sickness or death, he viewed the positive solution as the reality rather than acknowledging the negative evidence at hand. Jesus always related his positive thinking to a higher power.

Yet today, his followers do not follow his example. The majority of the Christians are taught by their leaders that sin, depravity, sickness and disease are negative realities that may be sponsored by Satan and are to be feared. They believe that loving Jesus as a personal savior is a reality to being saved. Death, they view as the great fork in the road between Heaven and Hell. Satan is (a reality) conceived as the great disciplinarian for all bad people who die.

Doesn't Christian logic indicate a different view? If negative circumstances are to be overcome, their unreality should be recognized and positive circumstances should be seen as supreme. Death must lead to nowhere other than just another obstacle to overcome. Shouldn't positive thinking include the abundance of love, intelligence, and the purity of thought to the exclusion of negative perceptions as realities? The view that God and Satan, along with good and evil, are both realities is a self-defeating dichotomy!

THE ATHEIST MAY BE THE TRUE CHRISTIAN

Both Atheists and Christians acknowledge that there are attributes of love, life, intelligence and truth that are extant. Christians recognize these entities as attributes of God. The Atheists recognize these attributes as part of self knowledge not related to a God under any name.

The Atheist doesn't believe in the story of Adam and Eve. According to Atheism, the universe developed through the process of evolution. According to the Christians, it was created by a magnified mortal called God, the Father, one third of the Trinity. This latter concept is refuted by the scientific community. This refutation is the result of intelligent, analysis of data gathered over many years by astronomers with their ever increasing technology. The biblical account of creation came from the tablets of the ancient Jewish nomads and were compiled in the King James Version of the Holy Bible in 1611AD. The Christian community believes that the biblical account takes precedence over scientific research.

According to Christian theology and their Bible, God created the universe and everything in it including Satan. If God is Intelligence, then is Satan the source of ignorance? Would the death of Satan transfer all living souls into immediate omniscience? Could this include atheists?

If Christians could reject the idea that Satan is the source of ignorance, then Christians and atheists could be on common ground in believing that the existence of ignorance is merely the lack of the knowledge. Is the Christian God going to reject the Atheist because he refuses to accept Jesus as his personal savior, or because he uses his God-given intelligence to the best of his ability?

There is absolutely no proof that the atheist, family man expresses less intelligence, life and love (attributes of God) for his family than the Christian. However, to the extent that the Christian rejects the Atheist's entrance into God's inner circle called Heaven, to that extent, he is less loving and maybe less tolerant than the atheist.

In terms of self knowledge the atheist recognizes his own attributes of life, love, and intelligence. To survive, he must use these attributes to the full extent of his being. He has no higher power to depend on. He must stand on his own. What he may not consider, is that love and intelligence are also Christian terms for God, and by his expression of them, he may become closer to the powerful universal laws of good (God) in the universe than he realizes.

Whereas his Christian counterpart, is a man born in sin. He is a helpless sinner who must plead for Jesus to intercede with God to give him a place in Heaven. This man may have a poorer sense of self-knowledge, because he believes that the attributes of life, love and intelligence belong to God and are disbursed according to God's will. Thus, he sees his limitations as ordained by God.

Maybe the basic differences between the atheist and the Christian are the attributes of self-knowledge. The foremost attribute of self knowledge is the concept of self-worth. There should be the view that as an individual born into a society should have something positive and unique to contribute to that society. This view adds the question of purpose to self-worth. Children aren't born with the concept of being sinners. They often in childhood ask the question, "what shall I be when I grow up?" Being a sinner is not in their vocabulary. Children are born with an innate sense of good self-worth and self-esteem. Sometimes there are circumstances in growing to adulthood that may destroy the belief in one's self-worth, but self-worth must be regained before there is contentment. Human beings will never be content with the world around them until they are first content within themselves. If a religious belief destroys that sense of a contented self-worth within an individual, then until that religious belief is destroyed, it will have a detrimental affect on that individual's sense of self-knowledge. Examples of this are the outcaste widows in India who are subject to the caste system. Their religious beliefs destroyed their sense of self worth.

The atheist doesn't see himself as lacking self-worth or as a hopeless and helpless sinner who must look for a power outside himself for redemption. The atheist sees that the amorphous entities of life, love and intelligence are within one's soul and are to be developed to the full extent of one's life for survival against failure and other various forms of evil. He does not believe in the so-called power of an entity called Satan. The atheist is solely responsible for his own success or failure. He, alone, is in control of his life. Does the old adage still apply? "God helps them; who help themselves."

The Christian is not always the one who is in control. Billy Graham states that man is a sinner, helpless to help himself. Unless God helps him, he is lost.

Christians believe in the power of two deified mortals--Jesus and Satan. They are two entities with no proof of present existence; yet, Christians believe that Satan can interfere with intelligent action. It is only through God, Jesus, can they be successful and saved. So in terms of not accepting religious mythologies as true and powerful, it would seem that the atheist may be a bit closer to God in thought and deed than the Christian Fundamentalist who acknowledges the great schism between himself and God.

CHAPTER V

GOD AND SATAN
GOOD AND EVIL ANALYZED

TRUTH

What is truth?

This is the question that Pontius Pilot asked of Jesus accusers. Were the principles of doctrine professed by Jesus, "truth?" Or were his accusers' long established rites, "truth?" The dictionary defines truth as "a quality of being according to fact." In the field of theology, truth is a quality of being according to doctrine.

One simple way to determine whether a fact, an idea, a concept or doctrine is true is to measure it against the qualities of truth. Truth is in part constant, eternal, immutable, incontrovertible, consistent, and indisputably verifiable. If that which is being measured is not congruent to these attributes, its falsity is exposed.

Today, there seems to be much diversity in Christian ministries as to the true theology of Jesus; so, why shouldn't the simple test for truth be welcomed? All religious beliefs should be able to withstand this test of verification. Truth is not subject to contradiction, nor change. Consequently, any view of God depicted with contradictory or changing qualities of character, such as changing from spirit to matter, or from good to evil, cannot be the true view of a changeless God.

The Inquisition in Europe during the 14th century was an example of how minorities suffered torture and death by a majority that were misled by religious leaders who believed in a fantasy not supported by truth. Now, seven centuries later, there is a question as to whether there has been any radical change in theological thought or in the thinking of today's Christian Ministers. Isn't the belief in mythological concepts and fear of the Devil still as strong as is the need to be saved?

Are we not seeing history repeating itself again here in the United States? Ask Reverend Pat Robertson or Reverend Dobson or hundreds of ministers of the Christian Right, if they believe in witches or in the reality of witchcraft. The answer may be a resounding, "no." In fact, they may condemn witchcraft as a myth or a cult. Yet, isn't it possible that future generations may question the current Christian belief in Creationism, Heaven, Hell and Satan. They contain the same qualities of myth as witchcraft. If the belief in God cannot surpass the qualities of myth and be indisputably verifiable as truth, then what basis does man have to worship any faith-based concept? Jesus with his healing works was recorded in the Christian Bible as a human man. So isn't human worship idol worship? Isn't the God that Jesus worshiped the same God that today's Christians worship? Didn't Jesus prove the existence of his God by his healing works? What happened? Is that God no longer around? Maybe Christians spent 2,000 years worshiping the wrong God. Can Christians prove that their present God is not a myth? Will their present ideology pass the test of truth?

In the meantime, there is a real concern regarding religious zealots who stir up mob mentality to commit acts of violence against any person or group that have opposing ideas to Christian myths. For example, can anyone prove that God condones killing doctors who perform abortions? If a married couple's expression of love results in an unwanted pregnancy, as citizens of the United States they have the inalienable right to privacy, personal freedom, and the right to have an abortion without the interference of a third party's religious belief. This includes the freedom to have or not to have a religious commitment, and also includes whether or not there is a God who opposes abortion. The "Pro-life" belief is in defiance of a world crisis in the over population of starving children.

The "Pro-life," "Pro-choice" argument in the United States is another example of the divisive nature of a religious belief that cannot meet the test of truth. This argument can polarize a nation and cause physical violence among its people. It is amazing that the "Pro-life" advocates do not realize that they are forcing a strictly religious concept on the "Pro-choice" segment of the American public. Their complete disregard for the life of the child, once they have forced a woman to bring a pregnancy to fruition, displays the hypocrisy of the "Pro-life" advocates. Do they provide food, care, and education for those children they force into life? Third world children are dying of starvation within view of the church that forced them into childhood. Is this the true love for an unborn fetus professed by the Pro-life advocates? If their God is "Pro-life," could He let children die of starvation? Can "Pro-life" advocates prove that the death of the fetus by abortion is far more stressful for both mother and fetus than for the mother and child to die of starvation after birth? Where is the research on this?

In the third world there are over 100,000 Sudanese facing starvation. In Mozambique, people eat grasshoppers which they name flying shrimp. In Haiti's slums there are swirls of dough that look appetizing until you find that they are made of salt, butter, water and dirt. In many third world countries facing starvation there are no pet animals. Are they the first to die? Near the end of the second world war Germans were eating out of the American Army's Mess Hall's garbage cans. There were no dogs or cats to be found. Starvation is a terrible ordeal for any living being to face. Starving women strap stones to their stomachs to lessen the pangs of hunger. Mothers boil stones and tell their children that food is cooking hoping that they will go to sleep while waiting to be fed. As the world population doubles hunger may become a common problem. For more information An Article by David Oliver Relin on this problem, read "Where food is not an Option " by Donald G. Mc Neil Jr. New York Times, May 23, 2004.

An Article by David Oliver Relin, Magazine. Parade section of the Seattle Times April 4, 2004, stated that more than 13 million children are in need of food in the United States, the richest country in the world. How many children worldwide are starving with no institution to feed them? The number must be staggering! Yet the "Pro-life" advocates seemed unfazed by the numbers or by the facts. They either deny that they are responsible for exacerbating the starvation problem, or they deny that the problem exists.

These are dangerous times for free thinking people. There needs to be a strong vociferous stand for the truth. For every single truth there are hundreds of possible errors, or lies, relating to that truth. The source of those errors is ignorance. Personifying ignorance in the form of Satan compounds ignorance with stupidity. Has any human being proved that the original source of evil or a lie is confined to one single entity called Satan? If there ever was a powerful Satan, why doesn't he have the power to protect the lie from the truth? The whole of Satan is the sum of his evil attributes. The destruction of one of his attributes (a lie) is enough to destroy the whole, because the whole is always the sum of its parts.

Isn't it logical that any entity that is opposite of truth has no power of action or ability to exist, either in the past, present, or in the future? Truth is such a powerful entity that it is defined as an attribute of God. When a lie, a mistake, any type of error, fraud, or misbehavior opposes the truth, it self-destructs. The truth may be perverted or covered up, but it cannot be destroyed, nor changed from being truth.

The truth and the lie (biblical terms for God and Satan) are easily seen as opposites. If the term God is equated to the qualities of good and truth, then the term Satan is equated to the concept of evil and the lie. The simplicity of this fact reveals that whichever is the reality, the other must be the unreality or a chimera--very frightening, but very unreal.

Sins, errors, and mistakes have no power against the truth. Because they are negatives, they have no principle to give them validity, and no God to offer forgiveness. Isn't it possible that the modern-day concept of evil and Jesus' concept of evil are diametrically different? The modern-day apostles see evil as Satan's evil--a terrible reality! Jesus viewed Satan as a liar, a lie and the father of the lie. In terms of absolute truth, the lie cannot exist.

Jesus and the prophets must have viewed Satan, sin, sickness, disease and death as intolerable options in the acceptance of the thought process that, consequently, rejected them as negative unrealities. In other words, the mental acceptance of the positive truth as a reality eliminated the mental acceptance of a negative error. As Jesus said, "Ye shall know the truth, and the truth will make you free."

THE LOGIC OF MISTAKES

The lie, an error, or a mistake, are all the opposites of what is true. For the "born-again" Christian, is a mistake not a sin? They both are the result of mental miscalculations. The fact that mistakes are unintentional errors does not change the effect of those mistakes. They will have a deleterious effect until corrected. If the Christian can correct a mistake, it should prove that sin is in the same category—not needing God's forgiveness to be corrected.

In the field of mathematics, errors have no single source of origin or powerful operating influence. Making a mistake in the application of a mathematic principle is not a blot on the character of the mathematician. The error merely distorts the solution until the error is discovered. The mistake has no principle to support it.

The general belief in past centuries that the world was flat, limited world trade. When the truth was known that the world was round and ships couldn't fall off the world commerce was expanded. The only power the lie had was in its belief that limited world trade. Once the truth is known, the error self destructs and becomes nothing.

Why is it, that today's religious thinkers do not apply the same type of thinking regarding an error in judgment, which they define as a sin? According to some fundamental church doctrines, man's inability to live without making mistakes brands him a sinner. Unlike the mathematician, the sinner is unable to be completely forgiven for his mistake without God's approval or forgiveness. The Christian must pray to Jesus to escape the influence of Satan who is the author and source of all mistakes. The Christian sinner prays that he can receive future salvation in a place called Heaven, the abode of God, a place devoid of sin or mistakes. In the meantime, current sinners have the satisfaction of knowing that Jesus died on the cross for mankind's mistakes (sins); therefore, God will forgive them for making mistakes.

This type of thinking can be self defeating if the mistake happens to be alcoholism, heavy gambling or some other type of self-destructive sin. If the sinner feels that Jesus has exonerated him, he may not believe it necessary to reform. Jesus will always be there to forgive his sin.

If this theory had been the standard thinking of the scientific community, it would have prevented centuries of scientific progress. Could it be that this   type of thinking keeps Christians from emulating their Great Teacher's healing works? If a scientist doing research work believed that mistakes were the result of some great power, too powerful for him alone to combat, isn't it possible that this false belief could generate too much frustration for him to proceed?   Scientists would still be in the dark ages praying for the scientific God to forgive their mistakes and waiting for death to redeem them.

Why do Christians make such a terrifying reality of sin? They accentuate the negative and instill terror of the Devil in their followers. Is this an intelligent approach to problem solving? Is it possible to learn without making mistakes?

If not, then learning may become a sin in the eyes of the Christian, because the Devil may use learning to generate mistakes (sins) in all aspects of life from birth to death. So is it possible that according to Christian logic too much learning may cause enough mistakes to land one in Hell? Evidently, the road to Hell could be paved with dead scientists including those killed by the Christian witch hunters. Or on the other hand, if God can forgive mortals for making mistakes, maybe with His great love, He will forgive all sins and give Satan access to Heaven. Thus, no one would have to die for making mistakes. To what ridiculous heights can mythological thinking lead? The most important aspect of a mistake is to realize that it is a distortion of the truth. Is the mistake in mathematics any different from a mistake in behavior that theists call a sin? Whatever the mistake, sin, or fault, it has no principle behind it; thus, it lacks the existence of truth.

Is it blasphemy to ask if there are any mistakes in the Bible? The answer is yes, if God wrote it. But according to history, a group of churchmen compiled the King James Version with its many contradictions—a breeding ground for mistakes. Mortals compiled the Bible and mortals make mistakes. This fact, even if it is only a remote possibility, should give great impetus to readers to avoid mistakes by applying logic, consistency and the qualities of truth to all Biblical passages. When a man admits that he is a hopeless sinner prone to mistakes, doesn't he defame his identity and defile God's creation? The fault is not the man! The man and the fault are not one! If man reflects the perfection of an infallible God, then man must be infallible and the mistake is not part of the man, nor inherent in man; thus, the old adage must still apply:

"Blame the fault and not the man!"

FORGIVING SIN

"Jesus died on the Cross for our sins" Does anyone really know what that means? Is there less sin in the world because Jesus died on the cross? If this is true, then how would one measure how much sin would be in the world if Jesus had chosen not to die on the cross?

Another meaning might be, because Jesus died on the cross for our sins, all who believe in him will have all their sins washed away before they see God in Heaven. This second interpretation would make death a desirable experience with Jesus eliminating all sins. Wouldn't this be an easy step to perfection? However, if life is the result of a continual struggle toward the elimination of a mistake or sin, how could death suddenly provide the elimination of a sin or mistakes without that struggle?

A third interpretation is that all sinners killed Jesus. Reverend Billy Graham believes that. In his book, "Peace with God", Page 99: "In the cross of Christ I see three things: First, a description of the depth of man's sin. Do not blame the people of that day for hanging Christ on the cross. You and I are just as guilty. It was not the people, nor the Roman soldiers who put Him on the cross. It was your sins and my sins that made it necessary for Him to volunteer this death." End of quote.

If Billy Graham believes there is a logical "cause and effect" relationship in this concept, it is difficult to ascertain how any sin today could kill a man 2000 years ago. If that statement could be proved incontrovertibility, then all Christians could be murderers. It is doubtful any Christian would want that interpretation taken seriously.

If there is a relationship between Jesus' death and cleansing mankind of sin, it is certainly ambiguous. Isn't sin strictly an individual problem that each person must overcome through trials and tribulation? How could the crucifixion of Jesus by an angry mob 2000 years ago have anything to do with eliminating the sins of present-day sinners?

Billy Graham stated that God's holiness demands that sin be punished. How does one punish a sin or a mistake? Forsaking a sin destroys it. Becoming aware of a mistake will often destroy it. What more can be done? If wrong-doing is the sin, just turning away from it will destroy it. Or does merely committing a wrong, warrant eternal punishment? If so, how hateful can the God of the Christian Fundamentalist be? It can't be the Christian God! The Christian Bible states that God is Love; therefore, Love is God. Love can't hate! Love can't punish or destroy! Love can't know sin! Love can only love!

Webster's definition of sin: A fault; an offense against God; a weakened state of human nature in which self is estranged from God.

Webster's definition of pure and purity: "Pure; free from taint, free from what vitiates, weakens or pollutes. Purity: the quality or state of being pure."

It is obvious that sin and purity are opposites. In the fields of music and the sciences, it is the purity of application that yields positive results. Purity of endeavor is absolute. There is no compromise, nor overlooking an impurity. Why would religious behavior be different? How could Jesus or God the ultimate of perfection in the eyes of all Christians, allow or forgive an uncorrected sin? Are the standards of musicians and the worldly scientists higher than the Christian God's standards?

There is an account in the Bible of Jesus saving the adulterous women from stoning. He did not tell her that she was a sinner and that her sins were forgiven, and now she could enter Heaven. He demanded that she sin no more. That is "forsake the sin!"

It should be obvious that forgiving sin can not be a cure for sin. Sin must be destroyed, not forgiven! A sin forsaken leaves nothing to forgive. A sin forgiven is not necessarily a sin forsaken. The view that God forgives sin is not an intelligent view of God; nor is there any proof that God forgives anything. Sin and evil are one. They need to be destroyed, not forgiven!

It is the Christian belief that Christian sinners who have met the criteria for God's forgiveness may enter Heaven, because Jesus' death enabled God to forgive their sins. This concept recognizes God and death working together to bring Christians sinless into Heaven. Isn't this a strange relationship for the source of life and purity to have with death and sin? Because of sin, one must petition Jesus at the time of death for a place in Heaven. Is sin such a reality that only at death and the capricious decision of Jesus, can one escape sin?

One common belief is that Adam made all men sinners which estranged them from God. To bridge the schism between God and mankind, God had Jesus die on the cross to exonerate their sins; so now they can cross the schism to Heaven. If the Christian ethic is to overcome sin, making it a great obstacle to God is not a very intelligent way to accomplish it. Why are Christians so obsessed with sin? Like any other mistake, sin will eventually self-destruct. If the purity of God precludes God from recognizing sin, on what basis is sin forgiven?

If one is to believe this Bible story of Jesus' death, why isn't it logical to have Jesus' death on the cross be proof that life is indestructible and superior to death? It is recorded that Jesus is the only man in history who overcame death. Millions of his followers state that the sole purpose for this great feat was to mitigate sinful behavior for Christians. They could, then, enter Heaven without being hundred per cent perfect. Or if God washed away their sins they could enter Heaven in a state of perfection. Both concepts lack logic. If death gives perfection what is the purpose of living?

Isn't it a travesty to associate "appeasing sin" (the forgiving of evil) as a primary goal for the resurrection, instead of the preservation of life? Isn't it obvious that if forgiving sin is the reason for Jesus death, then Jesus died to preserve sin, not to forsake it? Does anyone really believe that Jesus was so afraid that the sins of mankind would separate them from God that he let the Romans nail him to the cross? Where is the logic in this? It is recorded that Jesus healed blindness, deformity, leprosy, sickness, a sinning adulteress, and he raised the dead. Yet Christians believe he died to combat the terrible power of sin. According to the Bible Jesus taught his disciples the impotency of sin and evil. Why would he then make a reality of it? This view of sin is like a principal of a school telling his favorite teacher to kill himself so the principal could promote all his students to the next grade. Who would gain from this scenario? Not the students, they would be losers along with the teacher.

If this view of Jesus' resurrection was gained from the Christians' interpretation of the Christian Bible, then this should prove incontrovertibly that the same Bible can give contradicting interpretations. There are many passages in the Bible of Jesus exhibiting absolute power over Satan who Christians believe to be the prime source of sin or evil.

From one interpretation of the Bible, Christians believe that God is the source of life, intelligence, and love in all living creatures. Also, from their Bible sodomy is a sin. At what point do they reconcile the actions of men to the attributes of God? According to the Christian Bible, God is defined as Love. Wherever there is love reflected in love, there is God. God as Love, couldn't judge, select, nor condemn. The Bible text condemns and judges by having the mores of the compilers or mores of Jewish nomads inserted into its text. If the Bible is the authority for the thinking and actions of the Christian God, then it is very obvious that a

God of love could not condemn nor kill in order to stamp out adultery or homosexuality.

Is being born a homosexual an unforgivable sin? If so, who is to blame? Is God to blame for creating homosexuals? Could God forgive sodomy? According to good Christians the answer is no. Only if homosexuals change their sexual orientation, then may they be admitted to Heaven. Isn't this an example of Christian bigotry instead of Christian love? Some Christian churches recognize this and are accepting homosexual ministers.

If homosexuals express love are they not expressing God? So isn't it obvious that a God of love is not involved with the sexual orientation? Like the light from the sun, God must be the source of love in the universe. Is homosexuality really a sin? It is a difference. They all would rather be considered normal—born free of this difference! Does anyone have control over his/her birth?

The Bible is an inspired book of moral codes for a mortal society; however, can one argue that every moral law needed for an intelligent operation of that society is a law of God? Adultery has no place in a perfect society. But is it a sin against God? If an adulteress expresses love in her actions, that love is an expression of God. How could God be involved with marriage vows, infidelity, or divorce laws? These are laws of a mortal society. Laws were made by using God-given intelligence, but they should not be considered laws of God. All of God's attributes are terms for God. Each attribute is a pure law within that attribute. Each attribute has no voice, no will, no judgment nor an opinion in regard to the civil laws of man. Those laws exist for the benefit for man. So the extent of their use must depend on man, not God.

In the realm of religiosity thought, the violation of moral laws by mortals places them in direct violation with God and his laws; consequently, they are placed on the road to Hell as incurable sinners. Is it logical to believe that a sin or a mistake is beyond correction? The secular world works on the principle that most mistakes can be corrected by mortals; why in the world of theology do most mistakes have to be forgiven by God? Many theists offer the widely accepted concept that Satan and Hell are founded on the belief that many sins cannot be corrected; thus they are subject to eternal punishment. Is sin the only trait or part of the imperfection in man that religion is able correct? If sin is an imperfection, then sickness, disease and death must fall into the same category as sin--an imperfection in man!   An imperfection that Jesus healed--not one he forgave!

LOVE

Forgiveness is an act of love.   But that, for which forgiveness is given, is no part of love. Forgiveness could be an acknowledgement of an evil act. God, the term for purity, could not forgive evil without vitiating the attributes of love and purity.   For example, the forgiveness for an act of killing—the killing was no part of love.   So God could no more forgive killing than could Love be involved in the act of killing.   The Bible portrays God advising Moses to kill twelve thousand people of Ai after having him write in the Ten Commandments "Thou shalt not kill." Which statement does one associate with God?   If both are true because they are in the Bible, then God contradicted Himself and became the source of love and hate; which, again, brings up the question, can God be a combination of opposites and still maintain purity and homogeneity?

Christians, who subscribe to the literal translation of the Christian Bible, must consider their God the source for good and evil.   Consequently, this line of thought would logically place their Heaven and Hell together into one location, not two.   Hate would then become the counterpoise of love, and truth coupled with lies would become the amalgamation of one.   Is this good Christian logic?

The Bible stated that God is Love.   Therefore, all living beings, that express Love, must express God; for Love is God.   Otherwise, Love is some sort of floating entity separate from God and it is useful only when one isn't hating.   Love must be greater than the entity that expresses it; or else infinite love would be subject to numerical limitations.   A person cannot talk to Love, nor see Love, (in Heaven) Love cannot sit on a throne, Love does not have a favorite son called Jesus, Buddha, or other multitudes of Gods, nor could Jesus, a corporeal man, become infinite Love, which is God.

What is true of love must also be true of all the attributes termed God: Spirit, Life, Truth, Intelligence, and Purity.   These attributes cannot exist separate from God.   They are God!   When there are statements regarding God's love, God's, wisdom and so on, there is a tendency to separate God from the attribute expressed.   The connotation of God's wisdom separates God from the entity wisdom, and it portrays the concept of God as a corporeal entity expressing wisdom. A temporal, material entity cannot be a spiritual, infinite, eternal entity because there are limiting characteristics to corporeality. Love is not ephemeral, but it is eternally expressed worldwide in animal and human devotions generation after generation. The universal quality of love is not individually owned nor possessed. Its abundance is limitless and none can claim sole possession of it. It may be compared to a river giving life sustaining water to all living beings in the past, present and future, but none can posses it

The dictionary defines love as: "affection, or devotion between Persons." This affection and devotion is also expressed in wild life between the female and her young. The donor of love could never be the only source of love any more than the recipient of love could receive the total supply of love. In the Trinity, for example, the concept of God, as the Father, is the expression and the donor of love to His son. Jesus is the recipient and reciprocator of that love. Therefore, neither the Father nor Jesus can be God, because their existence utilizes only part of love; the whole of which is God.

It is obvious that the affection and devotion expressed between entities does not decrease available love; therefore, isn't it logical that there must be an infinite supply of love per entity. And God must also be a term for infinite love. Doesn't the Christian who prays for love from Jesus resemble a man standing knee deep in water praying for rain to fill his bucket? He is blind to the abundance of water at his very feet. A petitioning prayer for something from God must be a denial of one's ability to achieve it by using the attributes of God. Christians pray for Jesus' love without realizing Divine Love, God, is ever-presently available to fulfill every need. To receive love, all that one must do, is express it.

If love is greater than the entity expressing it, this must also be true of its opposite, hate. If God is a term for Love, then Satan must be a term for hate. It is obvious that both love and hate are amorphous entities without any material accoutrements. Theists, worldwide, recognize Allah and Jesus as two spiritual leaders utilizing love for their kingdoms while Allah advocates the hate of Satan for his adversaries. Why can't they recognize love as a positive force of growth, and hate as a negative force of self destruction? The Christian Bible records Jesus walking through the crowd that was set to kill him. This certainly isn't an example of man utilizing the mentality of hate. If this is an example of the power of love, it could be a panacea for world peace.

Is it conceivable that world leaders who read the Bible, the Koran, or rely on Shinto, or the Torah, have preconceived notions as to how their various Gods, think and act? By their beliefs, are they not making the attempt to solve world problems on a mythological basis of religious dogma rather than on an intelligent action based on love and mutual understanding between nations? The leaders of Christian and Muslim nations want love and peace for their people; so why is it necessary to achieve these mutual goals by war? Acts of love must be the strongest force for world peace.

In the concepts of Heaven, regardless whether it is the Christian Heaven, the Muslim Heaven, the Buddha Heaven, or whatever Heaven is contemplated, the underlying attribute of life therein must be a life without strife--a life lived harmoniously among loved ones in the pure atmosphere of love. Love must reign supreme within any utopian concept of the hereafter.

In the present concept of Heaven, the Christian God, Jesus and his Father, will be excluding non-believers. The Muslim, Allah, will be killing infidels, and Buddha will be hating Allah; so how loving can their Heavenly societies be? Isn't it reasonable to believe that a highly intelligent society will also be a very loving society? Consequently, shouldn't the attributes of intelligence and love be a cherished goal for all mankind to express in their daily living, as well as in international affairs?

How much time remains for mankind to recognize that one concept relating to the Gods of all humans must be a concept of love? If the Islam Fundamentalists have been told to begin a Holy War against all Christians and to destroy Buddha, an atomic warfare between the followers of all these Gods could very well destroy the earth and all living creatures on it. If religious zealots and fundamentalists feel assured of a safe refuge in their Heaven, how much love or real concern are they going to feel for the preservation of earth? Somehow, eventually, love must overcome hate to save the world. This will probably have to happen first in the realm of politics.

In the Christian Bible there is a statement attributed to Jesus that states, "Love your enemies." This idea must have been an important part of the Christian theology, or why was it used to contradict the philosophy of the Old Testament which was "An eye for an eye?"

William B. Fotheringham

WHY WAS WAR THE ONLY OPTION?

The United States (US) has a president, George W. Bush, Jr., who claims that Jesus is his most important role model. Would Jesus have considered war as an only option? His message was one of love. Did the President or his administration try a policy of love before hate in Iraq? Instead of using a threat of war for a regime change and weapons removal, why didn't our diplomats attempt to make a change within the regime with an emphasis on changing leadership policies? The allied forces already had the power to make positive changes not permitted under strict Muslim law--laws that still remain a threat to the freedom of all Muslim women. Will a new regime, as approved by the U.S., give protection to the women of Iraq? Or, as with many theological beliefs, are women still seen as inferior and not privy to the love and justice of their God?

It is well known by the administration that as a child, the Iraqi leader learned from an abusive stepfather that violence was a means to an end. Although he was a ruler who ruled with cruelty and violence, Saddam was only one man surrounded by many intelligent men as needed to rule a country. Isn't it possible that following the war in 1991, the United States foreign policy with pressure on the United Nations could have made an attempt to cure the Saddam problem through education, behavior modification, or peaceful removal? There was known evidence of the many problems in Iraq.

Saddam, his sons and close associates believed in the dark arts. Saddam depended on magician advisers from Japan and China with their supernatural powers for his every move. Iraq is a country that has been isolated from the modern world for decades. A large following of Saddam believe in soothsayers, and the occult with supernatural powers. This large segment of the Iraq population believed that Saddam had a magic stone that kept the U S Army from finding him, and that he would eventually come back and rule Iraq.

The more intelligent approach to disarm all religious combatants is to give them an invitation to the peace table to prove to the world that their God approves of their actions. Persistent attempts to work with terrorists with love and understanding should be more productive for peace than trying to kill them all worldwide. Instill in them the need to live and work together as people, not as Muslims and Christians.

Doesn't it seem strange that the United States has the technology to place a man on the moon, robots on Mars, and probe the limits of outer space, but cannot bring logical common sense to religion? Is it because the thinking elite in this country have religious concepts that are on the same level of mythological ignorance as the religious terrorists? Doesn't this say something for the educational systems in this country, or lack thereof?

Love and education were needed before a war in Iraq! This was a very backward country that the United States attacked. It was like an adult attacking a small child. The United States beat up on them in 1991 and left them bleeding; only, to come back in 2003 for the kill, or is it possible that this is a very necessary war to expose the extremists who have for years wanted to destroy our country?

In the opinion of the author unanswered questions still persist: Why did we go to war with Iraq when North Korea was further ahead with their nuclear program? Why was the need to go to war with Iraq based on one source of information from the Central Intelligence Agency (CIA). Why wasn't the dubious, new information on weapons of mass destruction in Iraq verified by the UN inspectors before it was used as a basis for propelling this country into its first preemptive war? There was reason to believe the inspectors were still in Iraq. Or if not, couldn't they have been returned? As leader of the free world, how do we justify this war according to our constitution? Maybe the war was used to ensure the United States a political foothold in the Middle East. Or the war could have been used as a means for the United States to have an influence in the control of Iraq oil? The Administration stated that when the war is over, there would be plenty of oil revenues to rebuild Iraq. When will the war be over? This is the year 2008 and there is no end in sight.

As Vice President of the United States, does Mr. Chaney also have a present influential role in the operation the Halburton Corporation? Why were no-bid contracts given to contractors in Iraq who had previous connections with members of the Bush Administration? Can this Administration prove that it is above the influence of corporate power? Or playing power politics? All of which are a violation of their oath of office. These are harsh questions for a president that may have precipitated an inevitable war at a time when the enemies of the United States were at their weakest and before they acquired the atomic bomb.

Whichever reasons prevail for this war, the problem of revival in Iraq begins with the unification of all religious groups presently fighting out of control. If this is not an all out civil war, it is very close to one. American soldiers are dying daily fighting insurgents who are fighting a holy war to save their country from democracy, and bestow theocratic control over Iraq. If there were ever the need for the separation of church and state, it is in Iraq. Is the present leadership up to the task with an over zealous Christian President of the United States and his administration who believe in government support for religion? If Christian religious mythology, as supported by this administration, becomes a role model for the government of Iraq, the theocratic solutions for the problems in Iraq may become a mess that no one can solve.

Instead of ignoring the plight of the Iraqi population in 1991, a policy of love would have considered the problem urgently in need of a solution. If the last 12 years had been spent occupying a defeated Iraq, it could have accomplished what the U S is attempting to accomplish now after a war of destruction in the year 2003. Doesn't it say something to the United States and the United Nations policies, when a country that was defeated by a massive military force in 1991, survived under the misapprehension that they won the war. Twelve years later, the U. N. is still weak and sitting on the fence of indecision, while the hawkish United States is attempting to fill the void with war and doing nation building--a U. N. role that the United States should relegate and have no part in.

To repeat, the U.S. had the ability and opportunity in 1991, to use its power and influence to help a defeated country under constant U N scrutiny to instigate changes. It might have been worth the effort to have tried. Otherwise, do we know the aftermath of violence? The use of violence doesn't seem to be a good method to cure violent behavior in individuals, why would it be the best method for nations? Without intelligent foresight, violence at times destroys the entity expressing it. At the present, more than 4,000 US soldiers have been the victims of this violence in Iraq. Is there any change from violence to love in the administration's policy?

The Bush Administration's solution to this war is to "stay the course" which is American soldiers fighting insurgents in Iraq. Any change to that course is labeled by this Administration as a defeatist policy of "cut and run" even though they admit it was faulty information that got us into this war.

A man's judgment is no better than his information. In this case it was a faulty judgment based on faulty information that resulted in the present course in Iraq. So isn't it logical that a faulty judgment would result in a faulty result?

All of this rhetoric about political policies, warring factions and wrong political decisions comes down to the simple panacea for world leaders to keep their negotiations focused predominately on a positive solution with love. Man needs to use the power of love to curb physical violence.

The military might of the United States, available to the United Nations, seems to remain a role of a policeman. War with Iraq should show rogue nations that the expanded violence caused by war is not a solution for problems, and it should show the United States the need to recognize the power of love and cooperation with all nations in its foreign policy as opposed to a policy of war.

Eventually, if this world is to survive, the United Nations must demand that every nation's leadership adhere to policies that enforce human rights and the recognition of the right to life for all living creatures. This would necessitate preserving the world environment as a mandate for all nations under the United Nations. The earth is the only home man and wildlife have, and presently it desperately needs universal protection. A God of love would not approve of the destruction this earth home, but how to save it is a problem.

In North Korea, the United States is facing a problem much like Iraq in that there is a dictator who is small, self-centered and scared. His life force is governing his country. He cannot allow dissent! He has made it very clear that protecting his regime is his passion. He is willing to negotiate with the United States on any issue except a regime change. If the hawkish United States Administration insists on a regime change without negotiation, or refusal to discuss the issue of nuclear bombs as a threat, then a nuclear war could be an option for North Korea. Let us hope that eventually, President Bush will consider following his role model, Jesus, and try love before hate and war!

In the past history of the cold war, the first step to peace has been to bring enemies to the negotiation table. This is a step that President Bush refuses to do. Why? How are conflicts resolved without talking? Sooner or later it must be done!

The U.N. is faced daily with the world's universal concerns, rights and special interests. It is the only organization available to save the world. But the U. N. needs to become stronger in order to keep nationalism constructive and in check while dealing fairly with each nation's needs. A policy of love without hate needs to be their mandate.

SPIRIT

In the Christian Bible, Spirit is one of the amorphous qualities attributed to Deity. The Random House dictionary defines: "spirit as the incorporeal part of man, the power of mind, energy, the motivating life of living beings." In any case, spirit is related more to a living force of life rather than to life alone. One may say spirit motivates life as intelligence motivates learning.

Does spirit exist as a reality opposite matter? Does matter exist as a reality in two forms animate and inanimate? Do these two entities plus spirit have equal realities? The answer to these questions relies on one's viewpoint of what the term "reality" embraces. If "indestructibility" and "eternal" are attributes of reality, then both forms of matter must be unreal. However to accept this premise, we get back to the question "Does the destruction (death) of animate matter destroy life?" The answer is "yes" if it is believed that life and matter are one. Otherwise the answer is "no." It depends on one's belief system. There is no proof of what occurs beyond death. The theme of this writing is that spirit and life are separate from matter, because of the limitations of corporeality.

Is spirit related to knowledge? Can man know spirit? Is spirit only in a category of belief? Knowledge is ratified by proof of its existence. For example, man can prove there is working knowledge in most fields of endeavor. university law schools, medical schools, department of sciences, mathematics, schools of music, and the building trades. They all teach how to work with knowledge. However, spirit is not so easily categorized. Some will argue that apparitions of people long deceased are proof of the existence of spirit. Unfortunately, apparitions cannot be taken to the laboratory for an objective analysis; therefore, they remain in the category of belief.

In the realm of Christian thought, Spirit and God are synonymous; yet, Christians refer to God as He or She. With a one-way communication from man to God, they revert to a corporeal Deity by talking to God as if God were an entity thought to be man. It is amazing that Christians see no inconsistency in this thought process. In the Christian Trinity concept of God, the Holy Spirit becomes some sort of floating entity separate from God, but within God, also called the Holy Ghost.

If the spirit of life is inherent in all things that live, and God is a term for spirit and life, then where there is growth in life, there is God. For people who believe in the Holy Bible, God is defined as Spirit, Life and Love. If Christians would use these terms only in defining God, they could have proof of their convictions that God exists as a spiritual force. To view the Holy Spirit in the weak confines of the Holy Ghost, a Holy Person, or a man-made-apparition, places spirit as a belief without proof.

Spirit coupled with life and intelligence must also be a motivating force for learning. The accumulation of learning is knowledge. The fact that knowledge is productive or destructive is irrelevant to the fact that it is the end result of intelligence. If intelligence, spirit and life are related to God, there could be an argument for God being a force of good and evil except for one important observation. Intelligence must be a good positive force only. Negative intelligence (evil planning) is like a mistake, like discord in music, an error in mathematics or evil behavior; they all have the same ubiquitous element of self destruction. And in the absence of principle and eternal existence, they are ultimately an unreality.

Logically, isn't Spirit the underlying force behind all positive attributes of love, life, intelligence, and learning? The forces that hold the planets in orbit have been attributed to the power of God. However, in the material world, it is the power of gravity that keeps the planets in orbit. To date, the power behind the expansion of the universe is still inexplicable as is the origin of the universe. However, to relate material power to God is to clothe spirit with finite, material, characteristics. Any true concept of Deity must be wholly spiritual or wholly material. It cannot be both, because opposite concepts cannot have the same attributes of truth. Spirit could be the powerful force in the metaphysical world, as gravity is the underlying force in the material world.

The enigma persists that inanimate matter displays no viable force, or intelligence; yet, dead planets in the universe move in a very precise orbit as if controlled by an underlying intelligence. From the material objects in the world to the galaxies in the universe, man has proof that all matter is on a course of complete annihilation, and this alone precludes the possibility of eternal matter or an eternal, material man-God, such as Jesus. So how do all living creatures fit into this observation? This introduces the premise that the ultimate reality of all life must be spiritual. If God is Spirit, then man as God's offspring must have an underlying, indestructible reality of a spiritual life. This would entail a material shell called body that needs to be cast off. As in the words of the old philosopher, "Thought is the stuff man is made of."

If all living beings express life, love, intelligence and growth, then they express the attributes of God. If they also express evil in thought and action, are these also of God? The early Christians answered this dilemma by creating two entities: one the source of good and the other the source of evil. Man then became a target between good and evil. These two antagonistic, powerful forces became known as God and Satan. As a helpless bystander waiting for the winner of one of these forces to take control, man awaits his fate. This typifies the majority of Christian thinking relating to good and evil. Under this prevalent concept, man will always be the victim and never the victor. As an offspring of a spiritual God, man should be able to utilize the power of spirit. Why can't Christian seminaries teach him how to do it?

Have the "born-again" Christians, who are on their way to Heaven, ever challenged their leaders for proof of their words? Spiritual healings were the accomplishments of their teachers, Jesus and his students. It would seem logical that before anyone believes in any leader, that leader should have credentials to prove his leadership. Why can't today's leaders and their followers prove their words with spiritual healings on demand? As Christian ministers, they refer constantly to the power of the Holy Spirit.

WHY PURITY IS A TERM FOR GOD

The term purity used in this writing is a thought, an idea, or a concept that is free of error. The absolute incontrovertible truth would be synonymous with a pure concept. The following are qualities inherent in the Christian concept of God: purity, omnipotence, infinity, omnipresence, omniscience, and eternity. God could be considered the underlying cause and consistent source of all good, life, love, spirit, and intelligence. These are very powerful, positive, spiritual attributes. If these are accepted as realities in terms for God, then anything to the contrary must be accepted as unrealities relating to contrary attributes.

In the realm of mathematics, principle is pure and unfettered with mathematical errors. Without purity of principle, our technology would still be in the dark ages. We would still be burning heretics and living in mud huts on a flat earth. There must be an underlying principle of intelligence and purity that enables humanity to progress in technology worldwide.

It is the purity of the harmony in music that allows no discord. It takes years of arduous study and application of principle to achieve a degree of the purity of harmonious sound. In all the preceding attributes, purity of principle is the attribute of strength, and to obtain the power of positive thinking isn't it reasonable to assume that there are definite principles of purity and positive thought that must be followed to obtain the sought-for results in hopes and desires?

Jesus taught consistency and purity in his teaching by posing the following question: Can the same fountain send forth sweet water and bitter? To obtain the purity of thought necessary to do the works that Jesus expected of his students, could take years of arduous study and practice in positive, pure thinking.

Positive thinking could involve removing from thought any facet of negativity regarding health, relationships, business, finances or world problems. Every negative thought would have to be replaced with the purity of the principle of good (a term for God). If this positive thinking were applied to thought as arduously as the mathematician and musician applies their knowledge, logically then, shouldn't good results follow? Isn't it the ability to understand how to utilize mental power to overcome physical conditions, the reason that Jesus stated "if you have the understanding the size of a grain of mustard seed, one could move mountains?" Obviously, much study and practice would be needed to reach that level of purity to understand the power of positive thought.

Without the purity of positive thinking, wouldn't any concept of a Deity, or its attributes, be of no consequence? Isn't it the constancy of purity in positive thought that leaves no opening for negativity to enter? It must be obvious that once negativity is allowed to enter positive thought, positive thought is neutralized. Isn't this exemplified in the Christian theology that recognizes the power of the Devil or Satan along with their omnipotent God? Wouldn't this exacerbate the ineffectiveness of sincere prayer to an omnipotent God?

Jesus took pride in the accomplishments of his students. They in turn reached the purity of endeavor to do the "works." Just loving and worshipping the teacher doesn't produce the purity of thought, endeavor and results required for student achievement in the secular school system. Why would it be different in the Christian system of theological thinking?

RELIGIOUS CONCEPTS VERSUS LOGIC

What is more important than thinking? Maybe on par with thinking is one's ability to communicate thinking in terms of truth. Truth may be determined by an individual's system of filtering perceptions, assumptions, emotions and the use of language as a means of conveying expressions logically.

Logic is a system of reasoning; it is a critical thinking process that identifies reasoning fallacies in other's thinking as well as one's own. Critical thinking has its basis in deductive and inductive logic. Deductive thinking is a reasoning process that begins with two or more premises and derives a conclusion that follows those premises. The basic method for analyzing deductive reasoning is through the syllogism

If statements made in newspapers, magazines and books, could be analyzed with a syllogism that was error proof, all printed matter would be more sensitive to the truth. If parishioners would use this critical thinking process to evaluate church sermons, TV sermons and basic church doctrines, they might discover aberrations of truth by an error free syllogism. This statement raises the question how is a syllogism made error free? Rather than elaborating on the mechanics of the syllogism, the problem of discussing subjective ideas with a critical thinking process is exemplified by the following example: The Bible states that: "God is Love." Therefore it can be assumed that God opposes abortion.

At first glance this seems like two very logical statements that could be made by any member of the cloth, but under a critical thinking process the first part of this statement declares nothing more than God is another term for Love. Love is an emotion that is verifiable, but the term God is not a verifiable entity. There has been no ground work established that verifies God as equal to love, or that God is an existent entity.

The second statement that, "Therefore, God opposes abortion," seems like a very logical follow up to the first statement. However, there is no relative information that connects the two ideas. For example, there is no verifiable groundwork produced that would prove: 1. that God is a verifiable entity, and that 2. that entity opposes abortion.

No person can prove there is a God and without this proof, every statement relating to God is a recondite conjecture rather than absolute, incontrovertible, verifiable truth. Every religion promulgates a doctrine based on faith. One definition of faith is that it could be a belief not based on truth. It is an axiomatic concept that faith in a man-God is accepted universally, but without proof.

Many religious pundits will argue that the Christian Bible is the word of God, and it provides absolute proof of God. This argument completely ignores the factual evidence that in 1611, a committee of church men were totally responsible for   compiling the King James Version of the Bible.

The anathema that exists among zealots that hold beliefs in a vast scope of varying religious doctrines is that their views are based on their finite, anthropomorphic concepts of God. Religious pundits do not take into consideration that the personification of Deity defines and confines that Deity to the boundaries of mortal concepts. For example, terms such as: God ordains, God will judge, God will punish, God told, God said, God sees, God hears, God will reject, God selects, God's will, God's love, God's wisdom, etc., are terms used constantly by ministers of faith; thus, confining their God to the limitations of a mortal and to mortal thinking.

It is a proclivity of a mortal to bond with those who have the same religious beliefs; thus, there is a polarization of theological beliefs and concepts within Christianity that prevents the expansion of theological ideas and concepts. Also, most of Christian theology is bound to the literal interpretation of their Bible which makes it impervious to the logic of common sense. In fact, obvious mythology is viewed as a truth that is beyond human intelligence or comprehension. The Trinity is an example.

If there is a God, shouldn't that God permeate the universe and be the one God to all living creatures?   Shouldn't that God be omnipotent, eternal, immutable, indestructible, omniscient, infinite, and the source of all life, love, and intelligence?   This concept must be beyond the confines of mortality, and would have to operate on the principle of good, because all negative forces eventually self-destruct. This concept, by its nature, could not be a corporeal idol subject to the idiosyncrasies of a mortal man. Instead, this God needs to be an applicable principle of laws that are recognized and available for problem solving. Eventually, there must be the same God for the entire world. It should be obvious that a universal God could not be Jesus, Jehovah, the Trinity, Buddha, or any conceived man-God, because the same concept of God must be acceptable to all religious sects beyond the limiting concepts of corporeality.

It seems logical that other then the weather and earthquakes the world is controlled by thought. The quality of life is determined by the quality of thought and not the other way around. For example, if the negative circumstances in life become dominate in thought, then the total quantity and quality of world thought receives a negative contribution from all thinking individuals whose quality of thought is determined by the quality of their lives.

It is the massive acceptance of negative contributions to the total world thought that exacerbates the destructive wars, careless use of the environment and disregard for the welfare of wildlife. It is only by the reversal of these negative contributions from all thinking individuals that this world can survive from complete annihilation. This negative reversal must start with each thinking human being.

In Seattle, on Thursday, November 16, 2006, TV Station CNN, carried a talk program known as "Larry King Live." He had a panel discussing the importance and results of positive thinking. There was a statement on the TV screen that stayed all through the program that read. "Your thoughts create your future." One member of the panel told how as a homeless person on the streets, he turned his life around by using positive thinking. He is now a wealthy member of the community. Another member was healed of cancer by positive thinking.

 Why is the power of positive thinking so difficult for the laymen of the world to accept? This panel suggested certain steps to follow in order to achieve positive results. 1. Keep thinking positive. 2. Be grateful for what you have. 3. Think on wants not needs. Concentrate on what you want. 4. Wish for good only. 5. Never give up on your dream! 6. Love yourself, think only of good health. Remember that the body will renew itself every seven years; so do not interfere with this renewing process with negative thinking or by medical pronouncements. Do not abandon yourself! Maintain your self-importance and your right to good health. For theists who look to their God for positive thought, should ask, "Is evil, sickness, disease or death more powerful than their God's power of good?"

Changes in life occur automatically. Daily, mankind is bombarded on TV with images of diseases, sickness, allergies, tragedies, accidents, horrors of war, hatred created by religious bias, the terrible power of evil, loss of income, lack of necessities, and so on.. If all these negatives are unconsciously accepted as irreversible truths, then positive thought is negated. Yet, without positive thoughts, man is lost; so common sense should indicate that the power of good cannot be vitiated by the so-called power of evil. All these negatives must be subject to change—truth and good are not.

If all the major religions of the world would accept these amorphous attributes as concepts for God, they would devalue anthropomorphism as a material point of prayer for all religions. It is the proclivity of mortals to pray to another mortal. One doesn't genuflect to love, life, or intelligence. However, to the extent that these attributes are used in one's life determines the progress and success that is achieved.

Can the pious Christians who are petitioning and pleading for Jesus to forgive their sins, really be aligning themselves with the source of all good? Wouldn't a mortal praying to a mortal humanize prayer? This mortal becomes a weak petitioner waiting for the gift of success. His strengths are predicated on the whims of a Great Person in the great beyond. Instead of dependency on Jesus, the view that there are strengths in the higher laws of good, should shift Christian thinking into a positive mode and eliminate stressful thinking.

To the extent that intelligence is utilized by the scientific community, means they are reflecting the source of intelligence. (an attribute of God) Applying that intelligence to cloning and stem cell research is all part of increasing knowledge--one small step toward infinite knowledge. If scientists believe in stem cell research, or practice cloning, will God's wrath be kindled on man? Will man once more be rejected by God for tasting the fruit of knowledge?

Are Christians so egotistical that they believe by continuing stem-cell research, man will become as knowledgeable as God? In all probability, if all worldly knowledge were increased a million times, it would still be just a speck compared to infinite knowledge. To believe otherwise, places limitations on gaining knowledge, and lowers the concept of God to the limitations of mortal knowledge and preferential thinking. One example of preferential thinking is the religious opinion that Jesus uses a selection process to send Christians to Heaven or Hell--two places where gaining knowledge would be a useless pursuit.

Religious pundits give God the credit for the creation of our solar system. It shouldn't take an astrophysicist to recognize patterns of creation that are in accordance with the forces that are ever-present in the universe. The sun, an ever-present source of light, heat and energy, shines on every planet, moon, and asteroid in our system. On earth, the air, the water, and the rain show no discrimination to recipients. The omnipresence of life, intelligence and love expressed in all living creatures should be an indication that the positive qualities that we term God do not select or reject certain recipients on the basis of their actions, affiliations, or beliefs.

In much of Christian thinking the positive force is God, and the negative force is a person in the form of Satan or the Devil. Satan is believed to be a constant instigator of evil and the only possible escape from Him is through a petitioning prayer to Jesus, as one's personal savior. Only in Heaven is one going to be completely free of the Devil's influence; consequently, the ultimate goal for Christians is to relate favorably with Jesus for a place in the Christian Heaven. Do Muslims relate with Allah for a place in the Muslim Heaven? Are there more than two Gods who live in several Heavens? Do all of these Gods recognize only one Satan and one Hell?

Is there a Heaven for each field of endeavor in the secular fields of psychology, mathematics, music, architecture, and other sciences.? In the sciences, the positive force is the intelligent perception of ideas and the negative force is ignorance. Intelligent perception is achieved through learning which eliminates the negative force of ignorance. Is Heaven the ultimate goal for all these fields of research so they can terminate learning?

In the field of theology, shouldn't theological concepts be as precise, as logical, consistent and as efficacious as are the concepts in the fields of mathematics and science? To portray God as omnipotent and infinite portrays all God's attributes as omnipotent, and infinite. If one views God's attributes as both, positive and negative, infinite and finite, spiritual and corporeal, as most Christians believe, then, in reality they have no God of any practical value. Isn't this the same as in mathematics, where the plus and minus of equal amounts equal zero.

For all practical purposes, shouldn't Christians acknowledge that their God's positive attributes are ever available to give them the powerful forces of good for the solution to their problems? To view God as anything less than a positive force of good, weakens the ability to use the omnipotence of positive thinking. As depicted in the Bible, wasn't it the purity of positive thought, devoid of negativity, that Jesus taught to his disciples? Isn't there a positive approach to religion that is efficacious as well as universal? In the realm of mathematics there is no principle behind one plus one equal three. On this simple observation can rest the whole principle of life and religion.

Religion should stand for laws of positive good. All evil, then, the opposite of good, must exist as the error of three in the equation of one plus one. Evil in all its forms has no principle to verify its veracity; therefore, evil has only the power of a mistake--the power behind the lie. There is no power on earth, or in the universe that can change one small equation in the principle of mathematics. The laws of mathematics are irrefutable and eternal; consequently, this must also be true of the characteristics of God. Without an underlying principle of good that we call God, there would be no basis for progress in any endeavor to overcome evil. Isn't the simplicity of this truth now buried in religious rituals, pageantry, and religious mythologies?

Isn't it possible that religions give lip service to the attributes of God as eternal, spiritual and infinite which are inconceivable realities with no point of reference for prayer? So theists give these attributes more tangible references for prayer such as: Jesus, the Father, Jehovah, Buddha, etc. In essence this reduces religious thought to idol worship.

The fact that all religions are founded by mortals on earth, who have made claims of direct connections to God, completely delude parishioners. Religious faith requires a certain level of gullibility in blind belief to exist. All forms of faith must have a basis in truth to give proof of their utility. For example, human beings express faith in their ability to learn and to accumulate knowledge. The truth of their faith is represented in their accomplishments. . Why shouldn't religious faith also produce tangible results as proof of its utility; otherwise, faith without results ("works") is rote or blind faith. Blind faith also has its basis in belief, but without the truth and confidence for accomplishments. As the number of converts in a religious faith grows, comradeship seems to overcome rationality; thus, allowing some belief systems to take on the cloak of truth as mortal idols become corporeal Gods.

It is important to reiterate that no person can prove there is a God, but man can prove that there are forces of truth, love, life, intelligence and knowledge that are universally available to all mankind. If these forces are termed God, then God should be universal, and positive, or even a God that the atheist and the secular community might be willing to accept, and thus take negative concepts of religion away from mythological thinking that is faith in beliefs without healing works.

THE CONTRADICTORY GOD OF CHRISTIANITY

A picture is worth a thousand words. Unfortunately, there are no authenticated pictures of God, so God must be described with words. The Christian Bible describes God as Holy, pure, spirit, love, vengeful, murderous, jealous, powerful, unknown, unseen, and in terms of both monotheistic and polytheistic entities (Trinity); however, God is predominantly described as monotheistic.

The Christian Bible gives so many conflicting views of God that it would seem wise for one who believes in God to take a common sense approach and use descriptive words for God that express homogeneity. Instead, most Christians describe their God in oxymoronic terms in order to be in agreement with the Holy Bible.

There are as many biblical contradictions describing God's attributes as there are describing God's methods of operation. The following verses from the King James Version of the Holly Bible delineate a few:

I. There is the version that God is Spirit and man is spiritual.

John 4: 24. God is Spirit and they that worship Him must worship Him in Spirit and truth.

Acts 17: 22. Then Paul stood in the midst of Mars Hill and said, "Ye men of Athens, I perceive that in all things ye are too superstitious.

Acts 17: 23. For as I passed by, and beheld your devotions, I found an altar with this inscription, TO THE UNKNOWN GOD. Whom therefore ye ignorantly worship, him I declare unto you.

Acts 17: 24. God made the world and all things therein, see that he is Lord of heaven and earth dwelleth not in temples made with hands;

Acts 17: 28. For in him we live, move, and have our being; as certain also of your own poets have said, "For we are also his offspring."

Acts 17: 29. Forasmuch then as we are the offspring of God, we ought not think that the Godhead is like unto gold, or silver, or stone, graven by art and man's device."

II. There is the version that God and man are not spiritual. That God is a man. (Walking in the Garden of Eden) He made a material man (created from dust) and God is a man who walks and talks. (Adam is a man created in God's image)

Genesis 2:7. And the Lord God formed man of dust of the ground, and breathed into his nostrils the breath of life and man became a living soul.

Genesis 2: 22. And the rib, which the Lord God had taken from man made he woman, and brought her unto the man.

Genesis 3: 8. And they heard the voice of the Lord God walking in the garden in the cool of the day, and Adam and his wife hid themselves from the presence of the Lord God amongst the trees in the garden.

Genesis 3: 9. And the Lord God called unto Adam, and said unto him, "Where art thou?

III. There is the version that God is Love

I John 4: 8. He that loveth not, knoweth not God; for God is love.

I John 4: 16. And we have known and believed the love that God hath for us. God is love and he that dwelleth in love dwelleth in God, and God in him.

IV. There is the version that God is not love. He is hateful and vengeful.

In the following verses, the Bible portrays God as a God of hate that is in direct contradiction to I John 4: 8. and in Deuteronomy 5: 17. "God Is love and thou shalt not kill

Deut. 30: 17 And the Lord thy God will put these curses upon thy enemies and on them that hate thee, which persecuted thee.

Deut 31: 17 Then my anger shall be kindled against them in that day, I shall forsake them, and I will hide my face from them, and they shall be devoured, and many evils shall befall them; so they will say in that day, Are not these evils come upon us, because our God is not among us?

Numbers 31: 1. And the Lord God spake unto Moses saying,

Numbers 31: 17. Now therefore kill every male among the little ones, kill every woman that hath known a man by lying with him.

Numbers 31:18. But all the women children that hath not known a man by lying with him, keep for yourselves.

Joshua 8: 1. And the Lord said unto Joshua, fear not, neither be thou dismayed: Take all the people of war with thee and rise up to Ai; see, I have given into thy hand the King of Ai and all his people, and his city and his land.

Joshua 8: 24. And it came to pass, when Israel had made an end of slaying all the inhabitants of Ai in the field, and in the wilderness wherein they chased them, and they were all fallen on the edge of the sword, until they were consumed, until all of the Israelites returned unto Ai and smote it with the edge of the sword.

Joshua 8: 25. And so it was, that all that fell that day, both men and women, were twelve thousand even all the men of Ai.

Joshua 25: 27 Only the cattle and the spoil of that day Israel took for prey unto themselves, according unto the word of the Lord which he commanded Joshua.

Exodus 21: 23. And if any mischief follow, then thou shalt give a life for a life,

Exodus 24: 25. Eye for an eye, tooth for tooth, burning for a burning, wound for a wound, a stripe for a stripe.

Leviticus 21: 21. He that killeth a beast, he shall restore it. And he that killeth a man, he shall be put to death.

Leviticus 21:23. And Moses spake to the children of Israel that they should bring forth him that cursed out of camp, and stone him with stones. And the children of Israel did as the Lord commanded Moses.

V There is the version that God is not hateful and vengeful.

The preceding laws of Moses are contradicted in Jesus' Sermon on the Mount.

Matthew 5: 38. Ye have heard it hath been said, An eye for an eye, a tooth for a tooth.

Matthew 5: 39. But I say unto you, That ye resist not evil; whosoever shall smite thee on the right cheek, turn to him the other also.

Matthew 5: 43. Ye have heard that it hath been said, Thou shalt love thy neighbor and hate thy enemy.

Matthew 5: 44. I say unto you, Love your enemies, and bless them that curse you, do good to them that hate you, and pray for them which despitefully use you and persecute you.

Habakkuk 1: 13 Thou art of purer eyes than to behold evil and canst not look on iniquity.

END OF BIBLE VERSES

Author's Comments

The preceding verses are examples of the many contradictions in the Holy Bible. There are many more contradictory interpretations of the theology that Jesus taught. Some modern-day differences and examples of the contradictory nature of Christian religious concepts taken from the theology of Jesus are: Protestants pray to a spiritual God as a He--person? The Catholics also regard God as a He, but they attribute deific powers to a "She" in the Virgin Mary. the Protestants do not. The Catholics have a after-death concept of a place called Purgatory. The Protestants do not.

There is a Christian belief that Jesus is an incorporeal God who had a corporeal body. They believe that God is always immutable, but sometimes mutable. God is Love, but He is capable of hate. God is the source of both life and death. God is an infinite, finite person. The Trinity is three entities in one God. God is too pure to know evil, but He must have knowledge of evil in order to destroy evil.

Also, Christian leaders see no aberrations of truth in the above, nor absurdities to the following beliefs: a snake that talked, the healing power of dead bones, in demons that take control of a human body, a mortal who had been sainted by other mortals, a God who grew inside of the womb of a virgin, a God who can hear the dead speak from the grave, a God who made women inferior to men, a God who was transformed into a mortal man called Jesus, a God who thinks, talks and acts as a mortal and must be pleased as mortal, a God who will return to earth and take all his followers back to Heaven, a God who has the destructive power to kill Satan in the battle of Armageddon or other eschatological beliefs, a God who governs by his will or plan, a God who is both mortal and spiritual and confined all the evil in the world to a fruit tree, a God who can turn a man into salt or dust, and there is the belief that Adam, was the cause of all the evil in the world. There are many more contradictory descriptions of God in the Bible.

All of the above represent mythological concepts in Christian litanies. Is it possible that educated adults consider all these beliefs to be factual?

The previous beliefs comprise the essence of most Christian concepts of God's character. But in the composite of all these preceding beliefs only the future offers utopia predicated on correct behavior as defined by biblical interpretations. Thus, most Christians have to wait for judgment day, death, the second coming of Christ, or Armageddon to receive final disposition from Jesus, their God. Every concept Christians have of their God should be held to the test of truth. There is an exigent need for the Christian religions of the "free world" to prove they are not just fairy tales.

LIFE AND DEATH

Presently, life has two accepted views: The first view is that life is not continuous. It begins at birth and ends with death. There is no hereafter. The second view is that life is continuous and it continues after death. Most human beings subscribe to the second view of life. But the majority of theists, who vision after-death life, believe in religious mythologies that defy logic and common sense.

VIEW ONE

There are people who believe that life is terminated by death, life begins and ends in matter. The sequence of life is birth, growth, maturity, decay and death. There is no afterlife. This view is very logical; we all have only one life to live. Life is temporary. Life begins in the egg or womb, and is dead in the tomb. This is the materialistic view of life. Life begins in animate matter and is terminated in that matter. This view witnesses life and death as present-day realities with verifiable evidence that death terminates life.

VIEW TWO

It would seem that the preponderance of religious belief is that life is not terminated by death. Life supersedes matter. There is a hereafter and life is eternal. This concept necessarily views life as an indestructible, eternal, continuing entity. Its source is also inexplicable, but it is attributed to a force called God--a term for the source of life.

Facts to consider: eternal is defined as: without beginning or ending, everlasting, endless. Eternal, when strictly used, describes that which in its nature is removed from time having neither beginning nor ending. The "time- concept" is the most insidious, destructive force in the universe. The material universe and everything in it is subject to time, and nothing can survive the ravages of time. Until man learns to break the bonds of time, eternity will never be anything more than an inconceivable term along with infinity. Time is a very limiting concept that governs without opposition. All living beings live by time and they die by time. It is inconceivable to consider life without time; yet, eternity is without time. So the earth's time must be a limiting concept relative to the size and revolutions of the earth.

The definition of eternal inextricably portrays all present life as an afterlife. All living beings are living their own Heaven and Hell right here on earth. Death, by this view, is only an interrupter of a temporal life span. Yet all living beings innately do what they can to avoid death that supposedly leads to an eternal life.

The concept of an eternal, spiritual life may be like a circle with all its life forms intact and harmonious, impervious to its being coated with an enigmatical, material life with all its destructive forces. Maybe Jesus had the insight to peel away these material forces as an artist would peel away an inferior, cover painting to reveal a far more beautiful painting from a master. However, the "continuing life" concept is fraught with unverifiable speculations, assumptions, premises and concepts that lack proof of reality. Thus fairy-tale speculations of Heaven, Hell and Satan can receive the same creditability as the attempts to give logical assumptions without proof. In any case, this writing will attempt to give an after-death purpose to life, that may draw more questions than answers. For example, in the explanation of the "eternal life" concept how does one progress from point A to point B without the consideration of time? How does one conceive of "infinity" without limitations? One concept is that man has to learn and live with time as another dimension in life. The following life after death experiences may, at least, question the creditability of the fairy-tale speculations.

There was a report of a doctor who died on the operating table and was dead for several minutes before they were finally able to revive him. During those minutes he said, "It was an out-of-body experience. Wherever he went around the hospital or out on the street no one could see him. It was like he wasn't there."

It was also reported in the British Medical Journal, "Lancet" that Robert Milham died of a heart attack and was transported to the hospital where a nurse removed his teeth and inserted a breathing tube down his throat, Eventually they revived him. Mr. Milham reported that all the time they worked on his body, he hovered over it and watched what they were doing. Later, it seems, he did the impossible! He identified the nurse who removed his teeth.

A research study reported in the British Medical Journal, "Lancet" by a cardiologist, Dr. Pim van Lommel, on 343 survivors of the near death experiences (NDE), 18% of them reported out-of-body experiences. These experiences, though impossible to repeat for study, or even as a remote possibility of being factual, shows us we are still in the dark ages in regard to life, death and the hereafter.

On earth, death destroys the old body. Is God involved in the death process? Is the immutable source of life also the source of death? The Christian Bible gives an answer, "Can the same fountain give forth sweet water and bitter?" What then is the source of death? Some believe that death is the most feared of the deadly triad of "sickness, disease and death." In terms of the ultimate reality: if health, life and eternity are true, then the evil triad must be its opposite--a lie. The lie will always dissipate before the truth; thus there could be a need for this evil triad to be universally recognized as a lie, because the power of the lie is proportional to its belief that is accepted as the truth. This view certainly precludes death as a true road to Heaven and life with Jesus,

Is the human life dependent on a material body, if God is life? Does God provide an eternal, material body that is in the prime of life in Heaven? If this is the modus operandi of God in Heaven, then an immutable God would have to do the same on earth? What proofs do advocates of Heaven have that all bodies in Heaven are different from the bodies on earth? Does the belief that everyone entering Heaven will have an adult, material, eternal body solve this enigma?

This concept raises the question, why is perfection so available after death and not before? Is this life the only life man has to live? Or if life is continuous, has man lived eons before birth? So now, is this life the end of the road before Heaven? Has man finally reached Heavenly perfection? Expert theologians, who have such certainty of life after death in Heaven and Hell, should have an answer with proof to this question.

There is no attempt by this writing to prove a specific religion as right or wrong. There is an attempt to bring rationality to religious beliefs and to explore religious concepts for logic and consistency of ideas. This is especially important for parishioners who are mentally captive to illogical and indefensible doctrines. Such as the theists, including Christians and Muslims, who hold the view that death can be completely eliminated through the act of dying into an eternal future life.

An analysis of present life may possibly give an indication of the demeanor of a future life. Does each life begin again as a baby with a new body and an empty brain? If life is continuous, then wouldn't the new-body-old-body routine go on continuously for eons until man learns how to escape it? Can there be life without a body? For just an instant after death, all entities expressing life must either die into oblivion, or continue with new bodies. If life continues, then in that instant between bodies can there be life without a body? If the material universe is temporal and life is dependent on a temporal body, how could life be eternal? If life is eternal, then obviously, life is not dependent on a material, temporal body. So, which is true? Life is eternal. Life is temporal. It cannot be both! At this point, maybe one should examine the logic of one's concept of life after death.

If the assumption were made that life continues after death, then one may ask for the purpose of life. Eternal life indicates that life never had a beginning nor ending. There must be more to life than just going through a cycle of being born, maturing and dying. If our present life here on earth has no memory of a previous life, then a future life after death should carry no memory of this life. Which brings us back to the question what is the purpose of living? It seems the most logical assumption for life, is the acquisition and use of knowledge.

Would the acquisition of knowledge be more important than the love and memory of human relationships? Popular concepts of death entail a means of meeting with loved ones in Heaven and continuing earth-born relationships. Is it logical that the elimination of death is accomplished by the act of dying into   perfection where one can raise the dead and walk on water? In order to live a perfect life, shouldn't it require individual perfection? The only certainty in the present life on earth is that there is constant change taking place. Can it be assumed that the underlying motivating force for change is perfection? Once perfection is achieved is there a need for change? Doesn't it seem logical that it would take more than one life-time of individual living to achieve perfection? Thus, does it defy common sense to assume that the "continuous life" concept endorses acquiring knowledge as more important than maintaining personal relationships? Attempting to find the logic in the forces of good and evil, of life   and death in this world seems to be a useless pursuit. Yet, to capitulate to concepts of Heaven, Hell, Satan and other illogical mythologies, offers no intelligent solutions with logical answers.

Perhaps the scientists in India started an approach that may begin to give answers beyond religious mythologies? In India, the scientists took two very young kittens and placed each in a separate room. One room was painted with horizontal stripes the other room was painted with vertical stripes. After the kittens were grown, they found that the kitten raised with horizontal stripes could not relate to vertical stimuli and the other kitten could not relate to horizontal stimuli.

From this experiment they hypothesized that humanity might be like the kittens in that they are hypnotized to life on earth as the only reality. Yet present life may be the unreality and humanity might be blind to an unseen reality--to a reality that life is constant, intact, eternal and not subject to death. Is it possible that this is a concept that Jesus had in order to overcome death?

In a quick study of the Bible regarding the prophets, the disciples, and Jesus, all we learn is their philosophy. We know very little about their parents, their relatives, their friends, their jobs or their superiors. All we know is how they applied their Christian philosophy (their knowledge) to the problems that they encountered in daily living. The most important element in the relationship the disciples had with Jesus was learning from him and applying his knowledge. There is no record of the disciples playing games, socializing at the clubs, going to church together, or worshipping Jesus. Their relationship was only about imparting and applying knowledge. If acquiring knowledge is man's goal, then climbing the ladder to ever higher knowledge in an after-death life would have to continue with new relationships and probably with more challenging life-time circumstances.

With the death of the body, whether the death is metabolic, cessation of all bodily functions or somatic, characterized by the discontinuance of cardiac activity and respiration, the death of the brain cells seems to destroy life and body. The observation of a dead body certainly shows no mental activity. Since medical science cannot substantiate the source of life in a body, it is difficult for them to determine the source of an individual's mental activity, or what happens to it when the body dies or it lives on life support, while brain-dead.

Is sleep a parallel of the death process? Sleep is a resting state in which the body becomes relatively quiescent and unaware of the immediate environment. During sleep, a period of rest and relaxation, most physiological functions such as body temperature, blood pressure, rate of breathing and heartbeat decrease. Sleep occurs in cyclical patterns; in each cycle of 1½ to 2 hours, the sleeper spends about three fourths of the time in so-called S sleep characterized by large delta brain waves without dreaming. The second stage of sleep is called D sleep or paradoxical sleep. Although the sleeper is deeply asleep, parts of the nervous system are very active and rapid eye movements (REM) occur. When sleepers awaken following REM sleep, they report they were dreaming.

While the body lies at rest the dreamer walks, runs and engages in numerous social and active events. The dreamer has no conscious awareness of his sleeping body. The body and the dream seem to be completely separate. In the dream, the dreamer's body moves with the thoughts of the dream much more effortlessly than when awake. The stiff joints, lame back, overhanging stomach and sore feet of the physical body never impede the movements of the dreamer's body. Could this be a glimpse into the future where man may move his body with the speed of thought, or without a material body? The movement of the material body entails physical fatigue; so it is unlikely that it would be able to move with the speed of thought, but there is a body that one holds in a dream. Regardless whether the concept is physical or metaphysical, the concept of man involves a concept of a body that is unrelated to the mental characteristics that make the man.

Whatever view of life one holds, it is apparent that an analysis of sleep indicates a mental activity that knows no fatigue, nor cessation. Whether mental activity could possible supersede death lies only in belief. Present life, entails all living creatures having a new material body at birth and an old body at death.

Beyond that, there is also an enigma of the universe to consider. One premise that present-day astronomers observe about our universe is that it is expanding with a force at a constant rate of speed (with possible accelerated rates found) to a time in fifty billion years such force will disintegrate into nothing. This is in conjunction with the discovery of the black holes in the galaxies that are so strong that our earth will be squeezed to the size of a basket ball as it is absorbed into the black hole. When a galaxy is completely absorbed, is there so much compressed energy in the black hole that it could possibly explode and expand into a evolutionary process of the universe that starts over again and again until it ends with nothing? This speculation is congruent with the concept that every material object including the material universe is on the road to complete annihilation.

This premise of a disappearing universe is the antithesis of the concept of an eternal, material life, but congruent with the concept of a material, ephemeral life. Could it be possible that temporal, material energy is the counterfeit of eternal, spiritual energy? If man goes through a cycle of death and rebirth, maybe the universe does also. If life continues beyond the destruction of a material universe, then it seems that life would be in a far different form than we see it presently.

For some reason in the "Sorry Scheme of Things" forms of life on earth have gone through drastic physical changes. The physical bodies of dinosaurs have disappeared leaving only their skeletons as evidence of their existence while thinking patterns of man have gone from primitive levels to technological and intellectual levels. Life forms on earth during the Mesozoic era have no likeness to present-day life forms; isn't it likely that all life forms may undergo drastic changes. Is it possible that with future knowledge, man may mentally outgrow his body? By observing the drastic changes in life forms that have taken place after the settling ash of Kracatoa or between the Mesozoic age and modern-day life forms, it seems difficult to justify arguments against evolutionary change. Whatever the future may hold, present life forms expressed temporarily in animate matter remain a mystery.

The life expressed by all living creatures must be either life after death, or the only temporal life a living being has. **How can life be temporal at birth and eternal at death**? If life is therefore continuous, it could not start in the Garden of Eden or logically continue in Heaven or Hell. It is easy to recognize that all creatures on earth go through a learning process for purposes of survival. Does the termination of this learning process occur at the point of death? Does the early death of a child terminate his maturation, so he lives eternally as a child?

The following premise on the importance of knowledge is predicated on the concept that life is eternal. Life and the acquisition of knowledge are two forces apparent in the universe. If man has eternal life, what could be more meaningful than acquiring the use of infinite knowledge? One aspect of history depicts knowledge as accumulating through layers of generations. Each succeeding century expands the knowledge gained from the previous one. Thus, knowledge is ever-present and available to all individuals. It is neither discriminatory, punitive, temporal, destructible, nor does it talk or listen. It does not have a will, or a plan for mankind. Each individual must use his source of intelligence to make his own plan.

In order for mankind to benefit from omnipresent knowledge, wouldn't there have to be ever-present life? Without life what use is knowledge? With evolving centuries, the latest accumulated knowledge is present only with the latest generation. This knowledge is the compilation of all previous knowledge of generations long past. Because of the death process, the foundation builders do not benefit from the advanced fruits produced from their labor and knowledge. In "The Sorry Scheme of Things" shouldn't the Wright Brothers have the privilege to travel on a jet? The nature of knowledge seems to discriminate against earlier centuries. From the standpoint of knowledge, man would have to live in the prime of life from century to century to benefit from its growth. This could happen only by the elimination of the death process. Medical science is presently working on that possibility. The scientific community views death as an obstacle to progress, particularly to space travel. Why isn't that anti-death thinking prevalent in the religious community? It was evidently prevalent with the thinking of Jesus and his disciples, and the early leaders of the Christian movement.

On earth, gaining knowledge is a slow and arduous process of study, investigation and research. Doesn't mankind's proclivity to gain knowledge indicate a higher purpose for man other than complete oblivion following death as advocated by view one? Without proof to the contrary, isn't it absurd to think that educated Christians along with their uneducated, third world converts, may gain instant omniscience through their immediate transfer to Heaven by death? This is the "born-again" belief that is presently promulgated by most Christian leaders.

Can the Supreme Being's knowledge be terminated on earth by death? On an individual basis, the answer seems to be yes. Each man's knowledge is terminated by death. From century to century, knowledge increases; so death does not terminate infinite knowledge. If the view of continuous life is considered true, then may it be assumed that even though memory is deleted, a portion of man's entity remains intact to continue man's progress in obtaining infinite knowledge? This view entails the premise that man has a continuous thread of life through all centuries of generations. With death, does man lose his short term memory, and also lose his specific, material, personal identification in a material universe? If so, what is left? Does man have two different entities: one material body that dies which was different from the spiritual soul that lives? The answer to that question, logically, seems to be no! The justification for that answer may be found in the fact that every living creature on earth has only one unique DNA. Wouldn't uniqueness indicate a single unit purpose for future survival? If living entities on earth are going to die into complete oblivion, like a pot of beans grown in the garden, why is there a different DNA per individual? Doesn't that indicate a sense of importance per entity that is not available to the Beans?

However, when the body dies with its DNA, does part of its DNA continue with future life? At the time of death, does it begin a new life as a fetus in a women's womb? With our present knowledge, in order to have the same DNA after death, one would have to have the same parents. Research on DNA is in its infancy; its future is exciting. If science has progressed to the point of re-creation, why should it abruptly stop because of egregious fantasies based on religious doctrines?

Whether man is material, subject to the destructive forces of a material universe, or an amorphous entity impervious to those forces, it should not be a present concern in man's search for knowledge. Future research will give answers to an open mind, unfettered with deleterious concepts of religious dogma. In a free society, scientific research should not be impeded by either religious doctrine, or political mandates. Present research reveals patterns of negativity that mortal man must overcome. The following are examples of mortal thinking: in place of love he accepts hate, in place of health he accepts sickness and disease, in place of self-discipline he accepts self-indulgence, in place of knowledge he accepts ignorance, in place of free thinking he accepts thought control and the bias of religion or ignorance, in place of joy he accepts anger, in place of generosity he accepts greed, in place of dreams of grandeur he accepts limitations, in place of wealth he accepts poverty, in place of friends he accepts enemies, in place of fun and laughter, he accepts drudgery and frustration. in place of dominion he accepts mental slavery. And what he doesn't accept for himself, he accepts for others.

The idea that man could accumulate knowledge and dominion through levels of living necessitates the premise that life is continuous. All of mankind have a proclivity to gain knowledge for survival. The prime motivation for progress is learning. Life without learning is life without progress. Doesn't the concept of Heaven terminate the need to learn and progress? If man progresses on earth through learning, why should it be different if man lives after death? Does death give infinite knowledge without learning?

Is there any other way except through knowledge for man to gain absolute control, first, over himself, and second, over his environment? If there is life after death, doesn't it seem that gaining knowledge would be the sole purpose in life--both before and after death? What could take precedent to gaining knowledge? Despite all the hate, wars, and destruction, knowledge is increasing at a very rapid pace. Doesn't this increase in learning and knowledge give a slight indication that in the "Sorry Scheme of Things" life may be continuous for the sake of accumulating knowledge?

Some of the previous, hypothetical questions and assumptions may seem to border on the absurd. Yet, what is more ridiculous than having a temporal life on earth until death gives theists eternal life with omniscient perfection in a place located in the sky called Heaven?

This raises the question, "has life on earth no meaning?" Once in Heaven, theists have a spiritual, infinite, incarnate, anthropomorphic, monotheistic God composed of three entities as their life companions. Is the concept that life is temporal on earth and eternal in Heaven, too sacred to be challenged for logic or truth?

The goal for most Christians seems to be a life of love and luxury in Heaven with Jesus. Is this the epitome of human accomplishments? Many people are living that life style of luxury on earth. What is going to change for them in Heaven if acquiring knowledge is not their goal? Have they no interest in the knowledge that may prove their complete dominance over tragedies, sickness, disease, and death? For Christians, is life after death in Heaven, a life of blissful ignorance?

CHAPTER VI
CONCLUSION

The following information regarding the history of the Bible was taken from the New Columbia Encyclopedia; Columbia University Press.

AUTHOR'S COMMENT

The traditional view of the Bible is that it was written under the guidance of God; therefore, every word in the Bible is the word of God. The interpretation of the Bible is one of the principal points of difference between the Catholics and the Protestants. Protestants believe that all individuals have the right to interpret the Bible as they read it. The Roman Catholic Church teaches that it alone may interpret the scriptures, and their parishioners may read the Bible only according to the interpretation of the church. Such interpretation is provided in notes to the text that appear in the Catholic Bible. These notes vary from edition to edition. They are the celebrated extant manuscripts including 4th and 5th century Greek text and fragments of scripture. The most ancient fragments of the Hebrew text are 2nd century BC papyrus of Nash.

It is interesting to note that all faiths recognize that the Bible needs interpretation. Most books do not need interpretation; so, why is the Bible an exception? Is it because it writes about God? If so, then all who read the Bible must conclude there is nothing definitive in the Bible that proves beyond a reasonable doubt what God is or what God thinks. Despite this knowledge, isn't amazing that so many denominations claim their doctrine, which is the result of an interpretation, is absolutely the truth about God? Taking all this in consideration then the old adage must still apply: "By their fruits ye shall know them."

THE CHRISTIAN BIBLE

The first great translation of the whole Bible was Vulgate of St. Jerome; a Latin version still used by the Roman Catholic Church. The Greek text generally received in the East is the Aramaic Targum translation of the Old Testament and the Greek translation of the New Testament.

In England, parts of the Bible were read in the vernacular especially the Gospels after its recitation in Latin. John Wyclifite was one of the first to publish and distribute the Bible in the vernacular. In 1525, William Tyndale translated the Bible not from Latin, but from Hebrew and Greek and this was the first English translation of the New Testament. Its excellence became the Authorized Version used by the church.

In 1539, the Crown, Henry the 8th, issued its first Bible that was written by Coverdale, a contemporary of Wyclifite.

In 1568, The Bishop's Bible was another Bible that was merely the recasting of the Tyndale's Bible. The greatest of all translations was the authorized version of the King James Bible in 1611. It was written by a committee of churchman and scholars led by Lancelot Andrewes acting as a amanuensis for King James.

In the 18th century, Jean Astruc, a French scholar, began an investigation of the Bible that became known as the "the Higher Criticism". This was a name given to the type of biblical criticism that was distinguished from textual or secular criticism. The aim of higher criticism was to apply to the Bible the same principles of science and historical records as was applied to secular works for which no claim of divine inspiration could be made.

Following Astruc studies, German scholars such as Johann Gottfried Eichhorn, Ferdinand Christian Baur, Julis Wheelhouse, in the 19th century studied the internal evidence from the available data of linguistics and archaeology. The primary questions were determination of authenticity and the chronological order of the different parts of the Bible, and the identity of the scribes.

Their findings were disputed among themselves and bitterly attacked by others who felt the purpose of their findings was to discredit the Christian

Religion. The term "Higher Criticism" fell into disuse and is not used by scholars of today.

In the 20th century, American biblical scholars combined to produce the notable Revised Version of the Bible in 1952, and it was immediately adopted by many protestant churches.

END OF EXCERPTS

Comment

One consideration that is lacking in an analytical perception of the Christian Bible, is the fact that the Middle East societies were as male dominated in biblical times as they are in the present.. Women were then, as they are today, second-class citizens. Those who rule today, use their bibles as justification for subjecting women to unequal justice under their laws. Some examples are: caught in the act of adultery, women are stoned; men go free. Women are deprived of education, work opportunities or equal status with men. A young woman pregnant before wedlock may face death by stoning; the male goes free. Recently it was reported that a Middle East judge sentenced a woman to be gang raped for a crime they could not prove she was guilty of committing.

Christians, who view their Bible as the word of God, must realize that the King James Version of the Bible is also a male dominated version. In the Christian Bible, men are in positions of leadership. The lineage of a man was always referred to as the son of the father. The mother was not named. Most daughters were ignored. The role of a woman was to give her husband a son. If a woman could not bear him a son, her husband was free to seek another wife who could. Whether the first wife was banned from the household or allowed to stay was the choice of the husband.

Polygamy was no problem in biblical times. Surprisingly, it is not followed today by most Christians who hold to every word in the Bible as the word of God. If God approved of polygamy then, how can it be a crime today in a nation under that same God?

If the Christian God is a God of love and justice, then common sense should indicate that not every word in their Bible is the word of God! Unless of course, they believe their God condones polygamy, the stoning and mistreatment of women by men.

READING THE BIBLE

The wondrous compositions of music, poetry, and art have been the result of inspiration. Most Christians believe that their Bible, like music, poetry, and art, is also the result of inspiration. They believe that the committee of churchmen who were responsible for compiling the Bible were inspired by God; therefore, every word in the Bible is the word of God.

Do parishioners and church leaders ever wonder how there can be so many different denominations of religious faiths when all these faiths are based on one subject, taught by one man and recorded in one book? Is there any explanation for this phenomenon?

Differing attributes as truth prevents the logical questioning of many of the Bible's inconsistent concepts. For example, is there any record other than the Holy Bible that God talked to anyone? Does anyone ever wonder why according to the Bible, God talked only to the leaders of the Jewish faith in the Old Testament of Bible? Doesn't it seem strange that God talked only to his Jewish offspring two thousand years ago, and there is no record of His talking to them, or anyone else, since? Is the Bible the only evidence of God that Christians accept?

Although there are many authors and publishers of scientific text books, the subject matter and basic principles are usually the same. Mathematics and science majors, who, are graduated from universities all over the world, work with identical scientific applications. There are not different sets of scientific principles or laws of nature that are unique to each university. This unanimity is also true in the field of music. But this is not true in the field of theology where diversification is rampant. Doesn't this indicate that somewhere in theology, there may be an aberration of truth?

Each church has its own interpretation of the Bible resulting in its unique dogma. How can this happen? The healing miracles that are recorded in the Bible have given this book such world renown. It was the miracle of healing (the works) as done by Jesus that distinguished him as a teacher and a preacher from all the other preachers of his time. Realizing this distinguishing difference, isn't it strange that most Christian preachers today ignore any healing requirement for preaching?

It is obvious that today's seminaries have no healing requirement. This makes one wonder who has the authority to judge another's qualification to receive a doctorate in theology--a license for a minister to interpret the theology of Jesus to his parishioners? If healing is not a factor, what is?

Biblical truths cannot be a factor, because ministers who have graduated from the various Christian seminaries, have their own denominational variety of truths. How many versions of Jesus' truths can be true?

If the Christian theology taught by Jesus is the truth, then like the truth in the principles of mathematics, it must have the same quality of immutable, incontrovertible, true set of theological concepts. Yet, among the Christian churches the theological concepts of Jesus' doctrine are as divergent as their believers. Christian churches are aware of this. How do they explain it?

The answer is obvious if the church clergy are willing to look at all the digressions of truth that are presented in the Holy Bible. Evidently, the Bible presents many of the conflicting ideas that were prevalent in the 16th century. The lexicon alone negates pure translation of the original biblical text when one considers the diversity of the Hebrew, Greek, Latin and Germanic languages. Also, the cultural contrasts could obviate pure translation of the original text if it did not conform to the mores and folkways of the translator.

So the question--how does one read the Bible for its truth? It comes down to one's sense of logic. There are so many viewpoints and conflicting statements presented, that it may be necessary for the reader to select an interpretation that fits his idea of God. This, it seems, is what the founders of the variety of religious denominations have done to cause so many divergent concepts of Deity. Each denomination is adamant that their concept is the truth.

It is difficult for most Christians to admit that not every word in the Bible is the word of God. So, one approach in reading the Bible may be for the reader to:

1. Compare the healing works in the Old Testament to the healing work's in the New Testament, and analyze the thinking that accomplished the healing.

2. Make a test for consistency of ideas, thoughts, and concepts in the thinking processes involved in the healing.

3. When confronted with an inconsistent dialogue of ideas list them in homogeneous categories and choose those ideas that are logical to the reader.

In the final analysis, a man's judgment is no better than his information. In the case of the Bible, a man's idea of Deity is no better than his interpretation.

Could it be viewed historically from the beginning, that a vast majority of the text has been incorrectly translated or interpreted? Man has relied on interpreters, teachers, ministers, and priests for religious doctrine. The inspired word of the Bible may be much more difficult to decipher than is presented by average clergy; otherwise, wouldn't there be more "works" taking place hourly in all the churches?

Whatever one perceives about the Bible, it is a book "extra-ordinaire" about God. Whatever inspires one person when reading its passages may be meaningless to another. Nevertheless, it has been said that some people have been healed by reading the original King James Version. To change one word of this text would impose an interpretation inherent to the theology of the new translators. There are enough divergent concepts in the original text without adding more. Therefore, the standard edition should not be an acceptable substitute for the original King James Version of the Bible. If Christians believe the original text was God's word, why did it need revising? Can man improve on God's word?

BLASPHEMY

There are certain members of the Christian faith who have read parts of this manuscript and believe that the ideas expressed in this work are the blasphemous beliefs of an anti-Christ.

The American College Dictionary defines blasphemy as: 1. Impious utterance or action concerning God or sacred things. 2. Theology, the crime of assuming to oneself the rights or qualities of God.　3.　Irreverent behavior toward anything held sacred. When Christians of differing faiths or denominations hold opposite views of Deity, is that grounds for blasphemy? Who decides what is blasphemous?

Many Christian organizations worship the Trinity concept of God. The Jehovah Witnesses do not. They worship one God, Jehovah. Are any of these differing beliefs committing blasphemy?

The Bible declares that God is Spirit (John 4:24) and God is love (I John 4:8). To circumscribe these two amorphous attributes with the idiosyncrasies of a man-God might be construed as an irreverent identification of Deity or blasphemous by those who hold sacred or cherish the Bible's spiritual concept of God.

Conversely, many Christians worship Jesus as God with his many mortal, physical characteristics. They believe that Jesus is a God who listens, talks, and determines rewards, punishments and the behavior for his flock. Some of his followers might find a purely spiritual concept too impersonal and unlimited, as well as blasphemous.

So it would seem that the term blasphemy should be used with great circumspection in viewing various concepts of Deity that differ from one's own viewpoint. In fact, tolerance and love toward another's religious belief and concepts would go a long way in eliminating all blasphemous actions and thoughts.

Why is one's religious belief so intimate or personal that it cannot be discussed or questioned objectively. The slightest disagreement in concepts of Deity invokes resentment, rage and sometimes acts of violence. Since the beginning of time, religious wars are as common as they are prolific. Is there an answer? Modern universities are making an attempt at reconciliation by offering classes in religious studies. Students study ancient religions and the Bible as literature. Whether they go so far as objectively discussing and defending their own concepts of Deity, will depend on the level of tolerance accepted within the university.

When universities push students to do an introspective analysis of their religious concepts, it will not be a panacea for quelling religious strife, but it could be monstrous step in the right direction to interfaith acceptance.

William B. Fotheringham

THE FIRST AMENDMENT UNDER ATTACK

"Congress shall make no law respecting an establishment of religion, or prohibiting the free exercise thereof, or abridging the freedom of speech or the freedom of the press; or the right of the people to peaceable assemble, and to petition the government for a redress or grievances."

The preceding lines of the First Amendment to the Constitution of the United States are very clear and forthright for a free society that recognizes the rights of minorities. It is interesting to note, that since its inception, it has been under constant attack by the very people it was designed to protect. It must require a certain level of an unbiased, free public education for a society to live comfortably under the First Amendment.

There is no attempt by this book to advocate religious apostasy. There is great concern regarding a religious movement that would force the teaching of Christian Creationism in place of science in the United States' schools. In the United States where religious freedom is mandated by law, all religions are free to exist and should be protected from ridicule and criticism. In return, religions should respect and adhere to the principle of the First Amendment.

How do Christian ministers and politicians who are advocating prayers in public schools, vouchers for religious schools, and taxpayer money for faith based charities have such complete disregard for the Constitution of the United States. They absolutely have no understanding of the importance of the First Amendment. Evidently, the school systems that taught them, no longer teach the history of the United States and its policies that made the nation great. This must be especially true in areas of the United States where the school system violates the First Amendment by allowing prayers in public schools.

The Christian Right's vociferous stand against a "women's right to choose" and those Christian churches who demand public dollars to support their religious concepts show no appreciation of religious tolerance or respect for religious freedom. The First Amendment guarantees the right of the Christian Right to promulgate their doctrine regardless of its beneficial or detrimental affect on their followers. The cornerstone for preserving freedom of speech is education. The First Amendment guarantees, within the law, the freedom of speech for the powerful and the weak, it guarantees freedom of speech for those with a negative doctrine as well as those with a positive one. The doctrine of free speech requires a level of intelligence that recognizes not only every individual's need for self expression, but also, the freedom to express it.

This freedom of expression also includes the right to express, or not to express, a religious thought. No government can require a person to have a religious thought. Yet there was national outrage when the California court ruled the term "under God" should be removed from the pledge of allegiance. The term God is strictly a religious term! A pledge is a solemn promise. When a U. S. citizen pledges his allegiance to his nation, he is not required to also pledge his allegiance to a religious concept. God is a religious concept without absolute proof of existence! Therefore, the choice of the pledge must rest with the one making the pledge. Otherwise, a religious mandate is attempting to control freedom of expression. To remember this, must we revive the history of the Inquisition? Back then, refusing to say "under God" could have been a civil offense possibly punishable by a death sentence.

The ideologies of cults that have culminated in mass suicide are absolute evidence of the fallibility of the followers of a dominate leader who has a misleading ideology. Whether they are detrimental to life or not, cults have protection under the First Amendment.

Christian religious zealots indoctrinated with bigotry and "God-authorized" violence, have bombed abortion clinics, and killed doctors in the name of Jesus or God. This type of thinking incites civil disobedience and would have no place in an intelligent society governed by the First Amendment.

Any Christian doctrine is divisive if it separates the Heaven bound, born-again Christians from the masses who have never declared Jesus as their savior. This strong doctrine is like a divisive cancer growing in a society that fails through fear or indifference to counter religious ignorance with cogent reasoning and intelligent action. However, as long as these organizations keep their actions within the bounds of civil laws, they have the right to lawfully attempt the destruction of the First Amendment.

Couldn't a strong belief in any unsubstantiated theology be the same as brain-washing? What difference is there from extolling faith and the brain-washing of prisoners in World War II? Today, there are over 100 million Christians who believe in a theology that borders on superstitions, and mythological concepts that cannot incontrovertibly be proven as the truth.

In fact, most theologians refer to their theology as 'faith based' that is, not based on incontrovertible fact or truth. Yet, many Christian leaders want their theological beliefs to be taught in our public schools as an absolute truth from their God.

Tax dollars are too precious to be spent on this type of exparte instruction that would circumvent a broad curriculum. Our founding fathers, having experienced religious persecution in Europe, placed great importance on the First Amendment.

Today, public schools are under attack. Public school teachers are underpaid, text books are outdated, equipment is worn, funds for advanced courses in technology are badly needed; yet, some Christians are condemning the public schools for not doing a better teaching job. Are these the first blows of the Religious Right's battering ram to tear down the public school system and destroy the wall that separates church from state?

The old adage, "No man will be free until all men are subject to law" may also apply to religion. No religion can be secure until all religions are subject to a law that separates church from state.

It should be obvious to any observer, that the First Amendment must be preserved as absolutely impartial with its freedoms--from the lofty speeches of Christian ministers to the lowly speeches of profanity and obscenity of street protesters they all have a right to speak their frustrations. Freedom of speech is the freedom to expound ideas! Regardless, how repulsive it may be to the listener, any attempt to change the Amendment would be a blow to the freedom offered by the Constitution. The remedy to curb freedom of speech that is detrimental to society lies with other laws, such as laws against treason, against inciting civil disobedience and so on. The following cases show the attempt to destroy or by-pass the First Amendment:

Debate Over "Charitable Choice" Stalls Charity Bill.

The legislation known as the "New Market Initiative" (HR 4923) would provide billions of dollars in investments to poor communities nationwide.

The House passed the bill but it was stalled in the Senate. The church aid component stalled the bill. The supporters of the bill attempted to pass the bill by attaching an amendment to repeal the estate tax. But it failed.

Why do some religious members in the United States Congress ignore the First Amendment? There is a constant effort by some members to introduce legislation to by-pass it? Do they believe our Constitution is a document against their God?

Isn't it amazing that educated lawyers responsible for creating laws that affect all of the citizens of the United States can be blind to the difference between a factual, efficacious law that guarantees freedom of speech and an unsubstantiated belief in God that opposes that law? There are religious leaders of the Christian Right who would rewrite the Constitution of the United States in order to insert their beliefs and convictions that they believe were relayed to mortals by their mythical God.

FLORIDA LAWSUIT CHALLENGES CATHOLIC RULES AT A PUBLIC HOSPITAL - Church and State, October 2000

The lawsuit against the city of St. Petersburg charges that the city allowed the Bayfront Medical Center, a public hospital that was supported with taxpayer funds to be operated under the tenets of the Roman Catholic Hierarchy in St Petersburg.

Under the directives of the "Ethical and Religious Directives of the Catholic Bishops," patients were restricted from receiving a variety of legal medical procedures including abortions, sterilization, emergency contraception and artificial insemination. Patients' wishes identified in living wills could also be limited if they did not comport with Catholic Doctrine.

Is there a doctrine of morality, honesty and tolerance in "Family Values" promulgated by the Christian leaders of the Right? In the year 2002, the president of the United States, George W Bush, espoused the importance of Family Values. Reverends Falwell, Pat Robertson and representatives of the Religious Right, agreed that Family Values were an important part of the Republican agenda for America. If honesty is part of family values, would not the use of taxpayer's money for religious purposes be dishonest?

Why is it that those family values do not represent an appreciation of the United States Constitution? Isn't the battle for freedom, tolerance and individual rights, as recorded in the history of the United States, not part of family values? If the Catholic Hierarchy (part of the Religious Right) in St. Petersburg, knew that they were representing a public hospital supported by public funds, was it honest for a large theological organization to withhold a service that was prescribed and funded with public money? Does their belief in God exonerate them from being honest?

When a public servant is caught misusing public funds, he is either dismissed from a job, fined, or given jail time. Is there a difference if it is a church or a large theological organization that pressures a public agency to misuse public funds? Both acts are dishonest. Is money more important than honesty?

Is it honest for the president of the United States to use the power of the presidency to illegally use taxpayer's funds for religious purposes? According to "Church and State Magazine," the president wants to give 30 million dollars to church charitable organizations. Evidently as an appointee of public trust, George W. Bush condones this illegal use of public funds. He has not been able to get the support of congress to pass his "faith-based" initiative, and until they pass it into law, the use of public funds for religious purposes is illegal. President Bush has advocated the policy of "separation of church and state" for the new government of Iraq. Let us hope that he learns the importance of that policy in his own country.

It was reported in the October, 2002 issue of Church and State Magazine that James Towey, Head of the White House Office of Faith-Based and Community Services is going to move ahead with the President's initiatives. The Dept. of Health and Human Services is already using its budget to finance religious social service programs.

As long as the First Amendment is the law of the land, it should be the duty of every citizen to abide by it. Any attempt to by-pass this law is an attempt to break the law. Why are the church-going conservatives of this nation who espouse family-values, so intent on breaking this law? Is breaking a law of the land part of the Christian Right's family values?

Is it tolerant for them to require all the family planning in the United States to conform to a religious mandate of anti-abortion laws that presently do not exist? Where is the proof for their convictions that their mythical God opposes abortion? Shouldn't common sense require religious beliefs to conform to the rules of truth and prove the authenticity of their God's abhorrence to abortion? Especially before they attempt to make the whole of the United States conform to their religious beliefs. Again, isn't honesty and tolerance part of family values or is adultery the only aberration of family values that the Christian Right condemns? Is the thinking of the Christian Right so impervious to the lessons of history that they cannot realize that the 14th century Catholic Inquisitions could never have taken place under laws separating church from state?

The following cases show how fragile is the wall that separates church from state. If a religious politician has the power to appoint a religious judge who doesn't understand that funding public money for religious purposes is wrong, it may set a precedent for the tearing down of that wall. Will there be religious wars fomented in the United States in a fight for the American dollar? The myopic Christians must realize the importance of the First Amendment,

It becomes obvious that if the judges of Supreme Court of the United States have no respect for the First Amendment to the Constitution, the United States Treasury could become the treasury for religious purposes.

THE FIRST AMENDMENT UNDER ATTACK

(Continued)
(Another attack)

SEATTLE TIMES
Friday July 19, 2002
By Tan Vinh

COURT: STATE CANNOT DENY AID TO THEOLOGY STUDENTS

A Federal Appeals court ruled yesterday that Washington State cannot deny financial aid to college students who study religion, because to do so, violates the First and 14th Amendment.

The 2-1 decision by a panel of the 9th Circuit Court of Appeals stunned the states higher-education administrators and constitutional lawyers. They are now trying to figure out the effect the ruling may have on the state's constitution's provision for the separation of church and state including whether this will open the way for private school vouchers.

The appeals panel ruled that it infringed on the religious rights of Joshua Davey when they took away his scholarship three years ago after he decided to study theology at Northwest College in Kirkland, Washington.

In 1999, Davey, a graduate of University High School in Spokane, Washington had been among the first recipients of the state's "Promise Scholarship," financial assistance for low-and-middle income students with good grades to attend any college in Washington including private schools. He was a valedictorian who scored perfect 800 on the SAT.

After he enrolled in school, he announced a double major in business administration and pastoral ministries which prepare students to become ministers.

The state Higher Education Coordinating Board (HECB) which oversees many state scholarship programs, took away his scholarship money citing a state provision that no aid shall be granted to any student who is pursuing a degree in theology.

Davey sued. He lost his case in the US District court, but he appealed. Two years later in ruling in his favor, the San Francisco based court said the state's scholarship criteria are discriminatory and suppresses a religious point of view. "We are quite surprised by the ruling said Marquis Gaspard, Executive Director of the Office of the HECB. This affects all financial programs. The state can no longer discriminate on the basis of religion."

In her dissenting opinion, Margaret McGowan, wrote this was not a case about speech, but a case about funding.

END OF ARTICLE

Author's Comment

In this case before the 9th Circuit Court in San Francisco, taxpayer funds were legally given to an individual to study religion. Does this open the door for persons who now want to become ministers and priests to have their studies paid for by the United States Government?

Can the Catholic Church now charge the United States Government for the cost incurred in training all the priests, bishops, and cardinals in Catholic catechism? Is the government now responsible for all students in religious seminaries? How dangerous is this decision?

After this opinion, it was reported that Mr. Davey felt vindicated. Does the fact that Mr. Davey struck a hard blow at the separation of church and state, also render him great satisfaction. Mr. Davey should live in a country where the state mandates a religion and where no freedom of religion is allowed. He could then have a better understanding of what he is attempting to destroy.

Christian Fundamentalists along with Islam, seem to carry an anathema against the separation of church and state. Another example of this is in Poland. During the reign of communism, the Catholic Church had no authority in governmental affairs. Many marriages were conducted successfully without the sanctification by the church. However with the fall of communism, the Catholic Church is now pushing for those couples to re-instate their vows of marriage within the Catholic Church. On the world scene this is an innocuous matter, but it does show how this huge religious organization is once again moving surreptitiously to usurp governmental authority and eliminate any possible separation of church from state. Isn't it strange that Islam's Qutb and Catholic Canon Law both have an abhorrence to the policy of church and state separation? On this issue, do Davey and Islam support the same policy?

The fundamental problem with combining church and state is money! Once the state supports a religious policy, that policy will become dominant to the detriment of all other religious and government financial concerns. No government or religion can exist without financial support! The prize for Catholicism and Islam is to, gain control of all governments and then their resources. At that point, no other religion can exist.

This is exemplified at the present with all the cities and states in the United States desperately needing money from the federal government to fight terrorism. However, President Bush instead of heeding their needs as first priority, he set up a 30 million dollar, religious charitable fund for churches.

This is a dangerous example of a religious policy illegally using government resources to the detriment of government needs. This is also a real hole in the wall that separates church from state!

The following excerpts from the Washington Post show how little respect, or appreciation, some government elected officials have for the First Amendment of the Constitution of the United States.

Every large city in the United States is incurring tremendous costs with the need to protect their city and residents from possible terrorist attacks. In order to do this, they need financial help from the federal government. The cost of the war on terrorism and the war with Iraq has placed a terrible burden on Federal spending; yet, you will notice that $30 million dollars badly needed by the cities will be set aside for the president's "Faith-based Initiative." which is a $30 million financial donation desired by 500 churches--a flagrant violation of the First Amendment with the expenditure of the taxpayer's hard-earned dollars.

GOP is using Faith-Based Initiative to woo voters! Office's officials have appeared with Republican candidates in tight Races.

The Washington Post
September 15, 2002

By
Thomas B. Edall and Alan Cooperman

Republicans are using the prospect of federal grants from the Bush's Administration's "Faith-Based Initiative" to boost support for GOP candidates especially among black voters in states and districts with tight congressional races this fall.

THE WASHINGTON POST
October 3, 2002
ROBERTSON CHARITY WINS
'FAITH BASED' GRANT
By Post Staff Writer

"Today, Operation Blessing International, a Virginia Beach Charity created by Pat Robertson, is to get $500,000 in the first wave of grants to be distributed under the Faith-Based Initiative which gives federal money to religious organizations that provide social services.

The $500,000 grant award to Operation Blessing is one of 25 to be announced today by Health and Human Services Secretary Tommy G. Thompson. The money comes from what the administration calls the Compassion Capital Fund which has $30 million this year."

Author's Comment

It is surprising that our Republican President, Mr. Bush, along with so many church organizations, is not aware of the need to keep church and state separate. There is a new organization named Traditional Values Coalition (TVC) that is aggressively soliciting funds for the preservation of Christianity and to promote Christian religious teaching in public schools, such as the Ten Commandments. This could legalize a movement by the Muslim community to have government support for Islam to be taught in all American schools. Christians must certainly realize that in a free country what is fair for one religion must be fair to all religions.

141

SUMMARY

In summation, the question arises: are six-century Christian beliefs incontrovertible concepts that can withstand the analysis of twenty-first century common-sense logic and the test of truth? The Christian answer seems to be: sacred, time-honored truths of God are not subject to human analysis, nor human logic.

Eventually, Christianity must face the question, is Christianity the truth? Comparing Christian doctrine to the qualities of truth should reveal answers that are simple and logical. There are seven Christian beliefs that cannot meet the test of truth or logic. They are beliefs in: Creationism, Heaven, Hell, Satan, Trinity, anthropomorphism and the Battle of Armageddon.

Creationism: The universe, Heaven and earth, were created in six days by God including the Garden of Eden with Adam and Eve. Eve's decision to disobey God was a sin against God in God's perfect world where there was no sin. According to the Christian Bible, all of the evil (sin) in the world was still confined to the tree of evil knowledge until God talked to Adam. It was after Adam's disobedience (sin) that evil was released into the world, not before. Does this make sense? Creationism must be an allegory without logic!

Heaven and Hell: Two locations in the material universe consisting of omnipotent good and omnipotent evil. They are perceived as eternal locations in a temporal universe without access except by death. There is a prevalent belief that death will provide good Christians an eternal, good life in Heaven, and non-Christians will live an eternal, evil life in Hell. The Muslim Hell will include all non-Islams and Christians. Satan is going to be a very busy man-ex-angel if all Christians and all Muslims are sent to Hell by Allah and Jesus. Who is going to be left to live in Heaven?

How could God, the universal principle of good, have a basis in mythology? If an omnipotent, omnipresent Christian God is purely good, then the concept of Hell must be a nonexistent, impotent evil. The concept of Heaven as a so-called chosen place for a selected few good Christians contradicts the concept of an ever-present, good God for the whole of creation.

Satan: There is a prevalent belief that Satan is the originator and source of all evil, which is the absence of good, Simply stated, if God is an ever-present good reality, then Satan has to be a non-existent unreality. The power of Satan is in the belief of a lie. The lie brings forth the untold answers to the questions, "When God kills Satan in Armageddon, what happens to all the Christians and Muslims in Hell? Do they become good Christians or converts to Islam?

Trinity: The belief that God is one God comprising three entities--two of which are Jesus and his Father and both encompass the Holy Spirit. By its definition, the Holy Spirit is different in nature from Jesus and the Father.

Different in nature signifies a change. God cannot be mortal and immortal, nor change from infinite to finite. If God is the immutable truth, God, then, cannot be subject to change; thus, the incarnate Trinity cannot have basis in truth.

Anthropomorphism: the belief that God is like a man. This is one of the most dangerous beliefs facing the United States today. The Christian God Jesus is a God who can express love and rejection. The Muslim Prophet, Allah, can also express love and rejection. Allah can reject Christians from entering the Muslim Heaven. Some of Allah's followers not only reject Christians, but they believe there will be rewards for those followers who kill Christians and destroy Christian nations.

Jesus, as God, has the same reality as Allah. How can Jesus save the world from Allah, when Jesus adheres to the philosophy of love your enemies? Are Christians, the followers of Jesus, going to disobey Jesus and lead the fight against the Muslims who hate Americans?

Armageddon is the belief that Jesus, or God, will gather his forces and go to war with Satan. Satan will be destroyed, evil will cease to exist and all good Christians will live happily ever after. It doesn't recognize where all the other world religions fit in this terrible war. Are they part of Satan's army?

These religious mythological beliefs are a threat to world peace, and they can only be rendered harmless by knowledge and truth. But who in the world is willing to challenge religious beliefs for their veracity? Instead, many Christians want taxpayers to support teaching mythological theology as the word of God in all American schools--public and private.

THEOLOGIANS ON TELLEVISION

Easter Sunday, April 20, 2003, on TV channel CNN, Larry King interviewed five renowned theologians of: Catholic, Protestant, Jewish, and Muslim faiths. Father Manning, a Catholic Priest, and a John Mcarthur, a protestant college president, cited the King James Version, along with other versions of the bibles, to substantiate their belief that Jesus is God.

Both of these men, along with the others on the panel, answered viewers' theological questions based on the fact that Jesus is God. There was only one member on the panel, an author from India, Doctor Deepak Chopra, who refuted their interpretations with logic. Yet, the unfounded belief in a humanized deity was prevalent throughout the whole hour, both from the viewers' questions and from the panel's answers. One exception, was Dr. Deepak Chopra's arguments against it. .

It is beyond belief that educated men are blind to the simple logic of common sense that God cannot be both monotheistic and polytheistic or corporeal and incorporeal. It is also difficult to understand why parishioners give money and credence to these beliefs without challenging their authenticity with common sense.

History seems to repeat itself. Without interference from civil authority, religious sects compete for money from converts. When one sect becomes dominant, there is a propensity for greed to take over and infiltrate civil authority for the purpose of consolidating complete dominance in propagating their religious doctrine. The rise of Catholicism in Europe that led to the Inquisitions, is an example of the consolidation of church and state with greed to inculcate their dogma. There is an attempt now by the Christian Right in the United States to compete with civil authority for tax dollars for religious schools in order to gain complete dominance in proselytizing and ruling with religious authority.

This writing questioned not only the Christian attempts to acquire illegal funding, but also, questions the irrational and mythological religious beliefs that are so detrimental to rational thinking. Mythological concepts are promulgated by Christian ministers as factual according to the Bible and legitimatized as God's law. For example, there is an apparent gullibility of a million Christians including members of the United States Congress, who believe in the reality of a talking snake, a spiritual God who listens, walks, talks, and shares his power with a person called Satan or Devil as the cause of all evil.

Educated Christians also promote the illogical and bifurcated view of the death process. They view death as punishment for their adversaries and criminals. For family and friends, death is a positive experience that will ascend them into Heaven. Has death formed an allegiance with eternal life to usher mortals into Heaven? Aren't Christians supposed to overcome death as their teacher did? So how could death be the only road to Heaven?

One step toward the cessation of worldwide, religious strife may be for all theists to give up anthropomorphism and join the scientific community for an analytical approach to determine the existence of God. Worldwide erroneous beliefs in early centuries such as the world was flat, the sun revolved around the earth, witches were real, people can be ruled by demons, and so on, were not easily forsaken by the majority of the educated population. However, over a long period of time, through centuries of studies by the scientific community, some of these beliefs have been largely forsaken--but not by everybody.

Despite the confusing views of Deity by many church doctrines, the United States would not be the morally strong nation that it is without its large network of church organizations. In times of crisis, people band together under the auspices of Jesus' love to help one another. All churches recognize God as love. As church members from childhood, they were taught the importance of love. As born-again Christians they are striving to be the best they can be according to the dictates of their beliefs.

Billy Graham has been very instrumental in bringing many people to his concept of God. Whether one views his concepts as logical or illogical does not alter the tremendous good he has given to his followers. Aside from the murdering zealots, there is less civil disobedience within the church-going population as compared to the non-church group. These church goers constitute a tremendous asset to the law-biding citizenry of the United States.

Criticism of church doctrine is as old as the belief in a God, and should be taken in stride with the vast movement that all churches are making toward a better life. There is no unanimity within the church network as to which is the true or correct doctrine; so criticism of doctrine outside the vast church network is, also, of little consequence.

Eventually, the scientific community may determine that the belief in God is a supernatural phenomenon postulated by theists to explain the inexplicable. The concept of a higher power entailed the origination by Christians of various phenomena composed of physical and metaphysical forces of good and evil that became enigmatic entities called God the Father, God Jesus, the Holy Spirit and Satan. Beyond the realm of religiosity, neither the schools of theology nor the scientific community can prove the reality of these phenomena.

So, why isn't there a consideration of the premise that all metaphysical positive forces exist as eternal manifestations of universal laws, and for every positive there is a negative? For every good there is an opposite. So what does it accomplish to personify these positive and negative forces in the mythological beliefs of two anthropomorphic Gods and a Holy Spirit? Or is the personification of these negative forces with the fear and potency of Satan, the Devil or demons reasonable? If man lives beyond death, why couldn't he learn to utilize and master these positive and negative forces for his eternal existence? Positive thinking is presently recognized in the therapeutic arts.

Positive thinking can be equated to mental power. The Christian Bible has many accounts of the prophets, Jesus, and his disciples using mental power to heal sickness disease, deformities, to overcome lack of food or drink, gravity, bondage and death. In our modern society we have hypnotists using mental power to control another person's action. That a healthy rabbit can die from fright is another example of mental power.

In a theater in Portland Oregon, the audience was asked to place their keys on stage in view of the audience. A psychic used mental power to bend those keys to their breaking point in view of the audience. Whether this was a trick or mental power, the significance of it is that the audience accepted it as mental power. Yet, in educated and uneducated societies there is very little credence given to the ability of mental power to change physical conditions. Scientists use their mental power to devise physical things to change physical conditions.

The fact that hypnosis can be taught as a subject may open the door for other possible uses of mental power. It is obvious that our schools are not teaching the use of mental power to refute the reality of mythology or the ability to apply logic and common sense to controversial religious concepts.

For example, the preponderance of Christian theology teaches that loving Jesus, as one's savior, will produce Heavenly omniscience vicariously at the time death. If Jesus didn't produce omniscience for the living, why would he produce it for the dead? How could the act of dying produce knowledge? According to the Christian Bible, didn't Jesus' omniscient knowledge eliminate death?

If Christian offspring are taught to ignore common sense logic and believe in the reality of fantasy, what kind of scientific minds will they develop? As one of the leaders of the free world in technology, is our scientific community in danger of losing a large reserve of young, pliable, inquiring minds to mind-stunting religious concepts? For example, from the 14th to the 18th century, superstition of witchcraft fell on many who were interested in scientific experimentation. This resulted in their persecution or death because of the beliefs in witchcraft that required punishment under the auspices of the church and civil authority.

From past history there is evidence that man has a proclivity to search for knowledge. If cloning and stem-cell research are prevented in the United States because of the deleterious influence of religious doctrine, that research will be carried out in nations where religion cannot interfere with scientific research. Will the people in the United States stand by and let the Christian community, with their beliefs in religious mythology, interfere with our scientific community's discovery and progress in the search for truth? Is the United States in danger of becoming a second-rate nation in technology because of the political power and influence of the Christian religion?

To assure freedom of education, national governments must assure freedom of religion as well as freedom from religion. As long as there is protection of individual rights by civil law in a free society, those rights should be immune from the deleterious affects of religious restrictions on new ideas.

Presently, there is a migration to the free world of hundred of thousands of people fleeing religious persecution, atrocities and domination by third world religious regimes. Eventually, this may become a world problem that must be addressed by the free world. The shifting of the world population to free societies may promote the simple solution of separating church from state. Once civil authority protects an individual's freedom of religion, religion will remain in its rightful place, and citizens of the world will remain in their rightful place.

In the millennium the world's religious leaders may begin to realize that there should be more to religion then citing their bibles and worshipping a deified mortal long dead in centuries past. Love is a force that every human being has experienced that is separate from a personified deity. Life is a force apparent in all living creatures as well as plant life. Intelligence is an ever-present force apparent in all living entities,. From childhood a man is labeled with an IQ that is below average, average or above average. Within these limits he lives his life. It would seem that the most important role in life is to break those bonds that keep one from leading a successful life.

Love, life and intelligence are an ever-present force to break the bonds of limitation. The Christian ministry is notorious for teaching that man is not privy to the wisdom of God. Intelligence is not selective. Why isn't it seen as available as the light from the sun? If mankind would recognize this fact, it would break the barriers of IQ limitations and raise man's self-image and self knowledge to reflect the intelligence of his maker.

The freedom any religion enjoys under civil authority must also be subject to, and supportive of that authority. The law of land must take preference over church law and its authority; otherwise, religious anarchy could challenge or overturn the residing country's system of laws as was done by the Catholic Church during the Inquisition and witchcraft periods. Without absolute proof, not only of the existence of their God, but proof of communication from that God, no church should claim that their God's authority supercedes the legal system of laws within their residing country. Again, this is particularly true of the Catholic Church that has been hiding the pedophile activities of their leaders in defiance of civil authority. All churches need to advise their congregations that they need to be subservient to civil laws that are free of religious bias.

Differing beliefs in God should not be a cause for war between nations. Yet today, the United States is at war in Afghanistan because Muslim extremists believe their Allah, hates Christians. How long will it be before all religions drop their beliefs in anthropomorphism--one of the big obstacles to world peace? The other big obstacle to world peace is the reluctance of theists worldwide to analyze their theological beliefs for elements of logic and truth. Unfortunately, religious beliefs without logic or proof are one of the causes for war.

There is a strong desire by the world for peace. The questions most often presented to theists worldwide is, "Why does your omnipotent God of good allow so much evil in the world?" The basic thinking behind this question is that God is a person who can disburse good and evil at will, and He alone has the power to destroy all evil. The most common thinking behind the answer to that question must be that at a time chosen by God, He will destroy Satan during Armageddon. Until that time, it is God's wisdom that the world should endure the consequences of a living Satan. The faith and logic in that thinking is in fairytale land. If the power of good is omnipotent, it must also be omnipresent. It is obvious that for good to be omnipotent, it must be devoid of negativity. For every single, positive truth, there are millions of negative, untruths relating to it. It is up to man to find the positive truth and hold on to it. The answer to the question, "Why so much evil," can be found in the question, "Why are there so many mathematical errors occurring daily?" The obvious answer to both questions is, "It is due to ignorance!" Stated another way, it must be the lack of understanding of what the term "God" really embraces.

For the sake of world peace, are Christians willing to drop the concept of Jesus as God? The belief that death will ascend the dead to Heaven incurs a great danger to Mother Earth. Islamic extremists may destroy the earth in killing their enemies, but they believe that they will have done their God's will; so they can live peacefully in their Heaven. If these religious killers should consider for a moment the possibility of the medical profession eradicating death--their only road to Heaven, they may be forced to reconsider their options before destroying the earth.

Will any religious group worldwide challenge their present mythological concepts with the test of truth? The answer is predominantly "no" Unfortunately, the great majority of people will die before questioning ingrained, primitive concepts of Deity and His mode of operation..

There is an urgent need for third-world religions to abandon the mutilation of women and their divisive concepts resulting from religious bias. There is a need worldwide to recognize individual rights within every nation before the spread of the displaced world population strains governments into acts of war. Religious reformation may be accomplished by either education or war. Let us hope that the option worldwide will be by education.

BIBLIOGRAPHY AND REFERENCES

"The Holy Bible, Authorized King James Version." *The Oxford University Press; New York and London; Printed in the United States.*

"The Holy Bible." *The International Version of the Bible; The International Society; 1820 Jet Stream Drive, Colorado Springs, Colorado 80921; Copyright 1994.*

"Articles Of Faith.": *The Gatewood Baptist Church, West Seattle, Seattle, Washington.*

"The New Columbia Encyclopedia": *Edited by William H. Harris and Judith Levy, Columbia University Press; Fourth Edition 1975*

"What The West Seattle Christian Church Teaches and Practices;" *One page brochure "Things to know about the West Seattle Christian Church."*

"Science And Health, With Key To The Scriptures"; *by Mary Baker G. Eddy; Published by the First Church of Christ Scientists, Publishing Society, Boston, Massachusetts. Copyright renewed 1934*

"A Guide For Confirmation Instruction": *the Congregational Church, The United Church Of Christ, The United Church Press, 1994, Cleveland, Ohio, Published 1994, Fourth Edition.*

"The Book Of Common Prayer": *Charles Mortimer Gilbert, Custodian of the Standard Book of Prayer; The Episcopal Church September 1979*

"Peace With God"; *Special Crusade Edition, Billy Graham; World Wide Publications. 1303 Hennepin Avenue; Minneapolis, Minnesota; Copyright 1984.*

"Articles Of Faith"; *Of The Church Of Jesus Christ of Latter-day Saints; The Desert Book Co. Salt Lake City, Utah Copyright 1984.*

"Statement Of Mission"; *First Lutheran Church of West Seattle, Seattle, Washington; Affirmed by Congregation January 16, 1992*

"Presbyterians Their History And Beliefs"; *Walter L. Linage, John W. Kuyendall; John Knox Press. Atlanta, Georgia; Copyright 1944*

"Knowledge": *Watchtower And Track Society; 25 Columbia Heights, Brooklyn, New York; 1984 Edition.*

"Peoples Padre." *Emmett McLoughlin. Beacon Press, Boston, Massachusetts. Copyright 1954*

"The Changing Face Of Christianity." *Kenneth I. Woodward; Newsweek Magazine; April 16, 2001*

"Cosmos, Earth, And Man," *Preston Cloud; Yale University Press, Copyright 1978*

"Dominion" *Matthew Scully, `St Martin's Press, New York; NY; Copyright @ 2002*

Church and State; *Barry Lynn, Editor. Member of Associated Church Press; Washington D C*

ABOUT THE AUTHOR

His educational background consists of a B. A. degree from the University of Washington, a teaching certificate from the State of Washington, and he was graduated Magna Cum Laude in the Master's Degree Program from Seattle University. Neither degree was oriented toward theology. The author makes no claim to be an authority on the Christian Bible, nor on past or present Christian Theology.

Now as he ponders, whether rich or poor, how could material living with its pleasures, its limitations, its discomforts and its old age be a reality of good, or be God's good creation? Ineffectual prayers made to mythical entities, affords no assurance for a present or future utopian reality. There has to be more to life than the way man lives it. Although lacking the finesse of a professional writer, this book is the author's argument for a higher reality.